THE QUARTER-ACRE FARM

How I Kept the Patio, Lost the Lawn, and Fed My Family for A Year

Spring Warren

Illustrations by "Nemo"

SEAL PRESS

THE QUARTER-ACRE FARM
How I Kept the Patio, Lost the Lawn,
and Fed My Family for a Year

Copyright © 2011 by Spring Warren
Illustrations © 2011 by Jesse Pruet, aka "Nemo"

Published by
Seal Press
A Member of the Perseus Books Group
1700 Fourth Street
Berkeley, California

Library of Congress Cataloging-in-Publication Data

Warren, Spring.
  The quarter-acre farm : how I kept the patio, lost the lawn and fed my family for a year / by: Spring Warren; illustrated by: Jesse "Nemo" Pruet.
      p. cm.
  ISBN 978-1-58005-340-2
  1. Farm life—California—Davis—Anecdotes. 2. Organic farming—California—Davis—Anecdotes. 3. Farmers—California—Davis—Biography. I. Title.
  S521.5.C2W37 2011
  635.092—dc22
                            2010036215

9 8 7 6 5 4 3 2

Cover and interior design by Domini Dragoone
Printed in the United States of America by RR Donnelley
Distributed by Publishers Group West

FOR LOUIS

CONTENTS

PREFACE

When my husband, Louis, and I were first married more than twenty years ago, we lived in a tiny student apartment in Connecticut. When the weather permitted, we hauled pots of dirt onto the concrete steps outside the back door and grew spindly beans up the pipe railings. When our sons, Jesse and Sam, were eleven and one, we bought our first house in San Diego. On the day we moved in, we planted two beds of tomatoes and basil before we even put our own beds together. Five years later we moved to Northern California and the whole family helped dig up the two dozen heirloom roses from our new yard so that I might plant fruit trees in their stead.

Gardening was a hobby, like making furniture or pottery. I enjoyed taking something that might seem worthless, old wood and clay (or a seed), and making it into cabinets and bowls (or eventually lunch). Gardening was especially good because the plant itself did most of the work of growing into a plant and then producing food. If I didn't forget to water it, that is.

It was great seeing the kids standing under a tree grazing on fruit, picking cherry tomatoes for lunch, or munching snap peas—especially because I knew that in our garden they wouldn't be ingesting chemical residues as they ate. When Sam toddled out of the garden scented by basil, I knew the worst he could have eaten was an organic caterpillar.

I dreamed of enlarging our garden into a place that we could live off of; a place resembling something between the Big Rock Candy Mountain and Eden. I thought about it enough over the years that it began to seem possible, albeit without lemonade springs or, hopefully, snakes. Years later while researching a book I was writing on World War I, I became intrigued with victory gardens, which the American government encouraged citizens to grow fruits and vegetables in whatever space they could find (yards, roofs, vacant lots) to help supplement family diets and feed overseas troops. I dreamed about how much my own small plot might produce.

I might have been content with mere dreaming, if not for the road trip we took in the summer of 2008. Louis and I had a conference to go to, research to do, and family to visit, which would take us on a meandering voyage from Davis to Los Angeles to Arizona, through Wyoming and North Dakota, and back home again.

It was a bad time to travel. Fuel prices were at an all-time high and when I gassed up at the pump, I felt like I was calling down environmental ruin. Furthermore, the fuel shortage coincided with a salmonella outbreak. Over 1,400 people were sickened by food-borne illness. The authorities thought the source was tomatoes. Suddenly there wasn't a tomato to be found on dinner salads, burgers, or as a garnish on the side of plates. BLT's became BL's, and summer lost its rosy culinary icon.

Then, just as you thought you were safe if you managed to skirt tomatoes, those same authorities announced that the source might be onions instead . . . or peppers. As the investigation went on, it became ever more clear that we might never know *what* food caused the outbreak.

Hence, food was constantly on our minds as we traveled. At roadside cafés we not only wondered what was on the menu but also how the vegetables had been grown, stored, and washed. And for that matter, how far the food had been shipped using our dwindling petroleum reserves.

On our way south we drove through California's Central Valley, passing the town of Coalinga, where the enormous Harris Ranch is located. We dubbed the town "Cow-a-linga" and steeled ourselves against the brick wall of stench we had to drive through to get to the other side of the immense feedlots there. The hellish crowding of animals was terribly sad and enough to make me swear off commercial beef. Knowing that the animals were often fed byproducts of other animals didn't help, especially since Louis and I had been in England eating meat pies the year that mad cow disease started killing people. The idea of eating prions from the tissue of sick cattle, then having those prions eat *my* brain, was a little off-putting. And where I once may have thought sick cattle wouldn't end up in my grocer's case, I now knew better. Activists had just aired film footage of dying cattle splayed out on the floor being prodded with shock rods, jabbed with forklift tines, and shot by sprays of water until they stood up and took their last tottering steps toward our kitchen tables. Large-scale meat and egg production was not pretty.

And still other issues with food were making headlines that year: genetically altered wheat, perchlorate in dairy products, transfats in baked goods. Hormones in our food were making some children grow breasts and body hair by the age of five; fertilizers, insecticides and herbicides laved produce we ate; and to top it all off, lead-tainted candy had been sold in stores. In short, what nourished us might also kill us.

Sitting in the passenger's seat of our rental car, with nothing but time to sit and think, I ruminated over these issues. It was time to do more than talk. I wanted to do what was right for the planet, my family, and me. As soon as we returned to Davis, I announced that I would start to grow most of our food in our own yard.

As I outlined my plans, Louis and Sam caught on that I was no longer woolgathering about a few raised beds; I was seriously plotting the transformation of our yard, our eating habits, and maybe the fabric of our entire universe. Louis and Sam paid sudden and nervous attention.

Louis said, "You're not serious. You can't grow your food in the yard. You'd starve."

As I noted the "you" rather than the "we" in Louis's comments, Sam pointed out that he ate responsibly while at home. Certainly—by the age of eight Sam shopped for vegetables at the local farmers' market.

Further, he researched companies for their environmental and humanitarian records and we made many of our food purchases at the food co-op in town where the checkers wear hemp clothing and the meat department is filled with organic free-range pork, chicken, and beef. I was the one in the family who was most likely to be caught eating a machine-extruded yummy pie laced with petrochemicals and wrapped by toddlers in a Malaysian sweatshop.

It was true that I likely had the most to atone for. (The road trip was even my idea.) However, I pointed out, we could all do more. The free-range chickens that we envisioned contentedly pecking in an open field are more likely living in a steel Quonset hut and seldom, if ever, going out into the concrete yard that constitutes their "range." Even health food—which might have been packaged in Pawnee, Nebraska, or Des Moines, Iowa—was likely to be aggregates of ingredients from anonymous factories in China, Mexico, and other far-flung places. Less than 1 percent of food coming into the country is inspected and the cost of shipping in fossil fuels is staggering. Even the food at the farmers' market, though local, has to be trucked into Davis from the fields.

Sam then said that perhaps I should wait another year to start since we were already well into summer. Louis pointed out that I was a self-described slacker gardener, after all, and I might do better with my plan after a bit more practice first.

I do hate weeding. I forget to water. My garden is a testing ground for plants able to withstand abuse. But while I seemed to have been a slacker gardener in the past, I explained that I was merely in my larval stage. The time had come to kick off my chrysalis and extend my farmer's wings.

When we got back to Davis I convened the family and told them what I planned to do. Starting on July 1, I pledged that 75 percent of all the food I ate (by weight) would come from our garden, hereafter known as the Quarter Acre Farm. The other 25 percent would be used as I wished on grains, dairy, meat, chocolate, or Boston cream pie. If I wanted to go out to dinner I could save up, banking the consumption of extra home produce to make up for it.

Gleaning would be allowed. If my neighbor didn't want the peaches on her tree, I could pick and use them. Finally, I decided that beverages would be exempt. Otherwise I knew I would not drink a glass of water, a cup of juice, or a swig of milk for the entire year. Also, I might be tempted to trade my 25 percent ration of chicken or cheddar for a good cold gin and tonic instead.

Lastly, I would be most happy if my family would join me in this venture.

Jesse was working as a line chef at the time, and he was gratifyingly enthusiastic about my plan. He said some of the best restaurants had their own gardens, not only because the taste of really fresh produce was amazing, but also because it was better for your health. On top of it all, growing your own food saved money as well. In sum, he thought it was a great idea. Of course, he didn't live at home anymore, so he could afford his enthusiasm.

Louis and Sam, on the other hand, looked crestfallen. I knew they feared being forced to take part in my experiment, to eat zucchini and chard three meals a day, day in and day out, until the moment, perhaps only weeks away, when they would simply keel over and (by that time, thankfully) die of malnutrition. They had a point. For while worries over pesticides, food-borne illness, and wasted resources were an uncomfortable sidebar to our century-long experiment with industrial global agriculture, and less of what we eat can be trusted than ever before, at least there was *enough* to eat. Louis and Sam wanted to remain assured of that.

For human beings, as for any organism that relies on food to live, famine is ever on the horizon and all societies are geared toward preventing that. The specter of starvation is what helped birth industrial agriculture and is what got us into this mess to begin with. Facing the reality of exhausted soils and diminished crops in the late nineteenth century, farmers turned to chemical fertilizers and synthetic pest controls. Mechanization became the way of things, and here we are.

"Enough" is the ultimate consideration of agriculture, and I could not expect my family to turn their back on that idea. They would come around, I was certain, once I showed them it could be done.

It was mid June. I got out the mattock, bought seeds and starter plants, and got to work on the Quarter Acre Farm, which—I hoped in the months to come—would be providing me with 75 percent of my food. I said I would go it alone; that Louis and Sam need not experiment with me. They could buy their food from the store. For *now*.

MAKING SPACE

"Show me your garden and I shall tell you what you are"
—ALFRED AUSTIN

With my limited yard space, every decision I made about what to grow on the Quarter Acre Farm loomed large. For guidance, I dug up a chart from the National Garden Bureau that ranked vegetables for their efficiency. The chart took into consideration everything from the plant's space requirements and productivity, to the resulting vegetable's nutritional value and store-bought price. The top-ranking vegetables were tomatoes, turnips, onions, lettuce, peas, beans, and beets. The lowest-ranked vegetables were melons, winter squash, and pumpkins.

I also looked at other charts, ones that ranked veggies on healthiness but did not necessarily agree on which dietary aspect was the most important. Vitamins? Antioxidants? Fiber? All the charts, however, concurred on one point: fruits and vegetables saturated with the most color were also the most nutritious.

I found this a little counterintuitive because I had spent most of my life associating the brightest colors in the grocery store with foods that were disastrously *unhealthy,* if rather tempting—bright pink Hostess Sno Balls, fuchsia Crunch Berries cereal, lime green Kool-Aid, and violet bubblegum, for example.

Ultimately, I created a ranking of potential vegetables that was a complex equation of my personal tastes combined with what I had any hope of growing. Luckily, there is not much I don't like to eat (including pink Sno Balls). Unluckily, I wasn't really sure of what I could actually *grow.*

I gamely listed tomatoes, zucchini, basil, beans, eggplant, spinach, chard, cucumbers, peppers, potatoes, tomatillos, and squash and then went to the yard to figure out where in the world I was going to fit all those vegetables.

There is a family feeling in our neighborhood, and as I wandered around my front yard, neighbors who walked by said hello and others waved from their cars as they drove off to pick up children from school or returned home from work. Even the circa-1953 ranch-style houses look enough alike to be siblings. In fact, if someone were to accidentally walk up the wrong path some evening (perhaps after a particularly discombobulating day at the office), it would be understandable if their first thought upon opening the front door was to wonder who had redecorated their front hall and put up another family's photos, *not* that they were in the wrong house.

Just as the houses are alike, so are the lots. And beyond a few tomato and eggplants, no one was growing much else in the way of vegetables. My own tomatoes and zucchini were cozied up beside the shrubbery and tucked like afterthoughts into the flowerbeds.

To live off my yard, however, I needed more vegetables than could fit with the cozying and tucking scheme. This meant making more space, which meant making big changes.

Looking out his office window, Louis must have spied the dirt-hungry look in my eye (and the shovel in my hand) as I scoped out the yard. With some haste, he shut down his computer and quickly met me outside. Hoping he could yet derail my plan, he made it clear that he liked the garden as it was. More, he said, people *needed* gardens for soul-replenishing activities like barbecues and sitting in the cool of the evening with drink in hand.

Looking around my neighborhood, I had to admit that my view of a garden as a place to eat from was far less common than the idea of a garden as a place to eat in. Most gardens are facsimiles of rooms with walkways, furnished with trees to provide cool, shady spaces in which to relax. A garden projects longevity. The brick and stone hardscape hints at having been there for eons, and a garden's crowning glory is the maturity of its plants, the visible care lavished on each one.

A farm, on the other hand, is comparatively hot and treeless. Vegetables, the most solar hungry of all plants, require eight to ten hours of sunlight each day; otherwise, fruit fails to ripen, leaves thin out, and plants become even *more* susceptible to pests and disease. Furthermore, farms tend to specialize in plants that are the mayflies of the botanical world; they complete their life cycle in a matter of months. As the seasons change, the plants die and are uprooted. The farm looks barren until the new seeds sprout and grow into verdancy.

In a relatively smaller residential yard, such turnaround can be shocking. A friend coming to visit just after I had pulled my frost-blighted tomatoes from their beds was horrified. "What *happened* to your garden?" she said, perhaps imagining garden-hating juvenile delinquents razing my greenery. I had to wonder, if this were *her* reaction, what would the neighbors think about my farming plans?

Farms, of course, have few people per acre, which means fewer people to mind if your yard brings down property values. In some part, that's why residential gardens have a history of restrictions.

The first neighborhood covenants, grimly racist, were put into place in the early 1900s, purportedly to increase real estate values by barring sales or rentals of homes to nonwhites. Today, in my town of Davis, the covenants prohibit things as varied as the color you may paint your house to the types of vehicles you can park on the street. I searched through the city ordinances and found a clause stating that "landscaping shall be provided to enhance the residential character of the zone . . . to include the preservation of all trees and landscaping including lawns where appropriate to maintain residential character."

I took some comfort in the vague language therein—who was to say what the residential character was anyway? What were "enhancements," and which guidelines deemed something appropriate? Vagaries or no, I was quickly coming to understand that growing my own food on my own lot in the quadrant P-12 residential zoning area was not going to be as simple as plowing up the quarter acre and sowing seeds. To both live in the city and grow my own food would require juggling what seemed conflicting requirements of my family, my town, and the needs of the farm.

So, while assuring my disgruntled spouse that we could still have a nice garden (just a slightly different sort than what we'd been used to) to sit in and sip gin, the two of us sat down with a rough map of our quarter-acre lot and discussed what we *could* change in our yard.

I made the first salvo, maintaining that the "residential character" of our neighborhood was varied enough that we could safely ditch the lawn.

Louis said, "We need the lawn for Sam to run around on."

I gave my spouse an incredulous look. Even when Sam was a darling baby, with an incredibly heart-melting baby façade, underneath it all he was actually a serious forty-five-year-old scholar. Thinking of Sam dashing about on the lawn was akin to imagining cats vacuuming. If there were to be any frolicking, it wouldn't be done by Sam.

I pointed to the driveway. Louis insisted, "We have to keep it. There are rules about the number of parking spots needed for each house."

In a brilliant sidelong offensive I said, "There are no rules governing *patios*, however."

Louis, not to be outflanked, responded, "The fishpond patio has to stay. We eat bagels there on weekends. We barbecue on the back patio, and you can't touch the patio under the olive tree unless you have a problem with reading books in hammocks on summer afternoons."

"Well," I said, realizing my options were quickly narrowing, "then we're deep-sixing the nonfood greenery."

"Oh?" Louis asked. "Don't you think that other people would consider that a visual blight?"

We both paused, thinking the same thought. We didn't want to upset our neighbors. Because along with a few cats, some rabbits, a duck, and a turtle or two, we also own two geese. And the geese, it turns out, are a problem—a potential *neighborly* problem, not to mention a personal one. First, we've had to fence them in (taking a good chunk out of our arable land) because the geese—a gander named Goosteau and his mate, Jeannette Pepin—are likely to bite anyone who enters their arena. Even though goose beaks *look* like they're made of harmless orange rubber, they're actually sharply serrated. Having a goose bite you is like being chewed on by a pair of pliers. The beaks also make the geese capable of defoliating a Guatemalan rainforest. Given the chance, they would deracinate every plant in our garden within a week.

Worst of all, our geese are two of the most hideously noisy animals on the face of the planet and that gives the neighbors power over us. Up to that point, our neighbors had been forgiving. I once asked Dorothy, who lived just to the south of us, if the goose honking bothered her. Dorothy, who was ninety-two, (we hoped hard of hearing), and so sweetly polite she'd send a thank you note for a tooth extraction, said, "Oh . . . there are worse noises in the world, dear."

The neighbors behind us reported they'd been raised on a farm and the geese made them feel at home. Our neighbors to the north, luckily, had barky dogs, were easy-going, and perhaps because they were schoolteachers, were used to a god-awful din. Yet we knew a single noise complaint from a disgruntled neighbor could force us to get rid of Goosteau and Jeannette because trying to shush geese is like asking night not to fall—it might happen in a few places once a year, but not where I live.

I quickly agreed with Louis. We had to keep the place looking pretty. The shrubs and flowers would stay if possible, and those that had to come out would be yanked a few at a time.

"If you really need to get rid of something," my husband offered, "I could empty the hot tub."

I was horrified. "I have arthritis," I hissed. "That hot tub is *medicinal*."

At an impasse, we decided to look *upward* for more gardening space. As it was, we had too much shade in our yard. In the front of our property, we had an immense city-owned elm tree. It was draped with so much mistletoe that total strangers made December pilgrimages to our yard for holiday decorations.

In the back of our house, we had a towering sycamore and two lines of fruit trees. The fruit trees were welcome on the farm, but our neighbors behind us had a row of hackberry trees planted on their fence line that threw a good portion of our backyard into deep afternoon shade. This caused the little fruit trees to grow bent at the waist, yearning toward the sun.

Louis told me he would prune all but the fruit trees to let in more sun. We started with the sycamore, cutting all the branches from the trunk as high up as Louis could reach with the telescoping tree saw.

This gave the tree a leggy-model look—long and lean, with a wild hairdo atop. The tree had just enough canopy left to cast but a lollipop of shade, mostly on our roof in the late afternoon.

Then I got lucky. When I requested the city trim the mistletoe and dead branches from the street-side tree, they informed me it was slated for removal because of the parasitic mistletoe and its advanced age. I got lucky again when my neighbors to the back cut down all their trees along the fence line to curtail the morning shade it cast in *their* yard. Within two weeks, not only did my yard's sunlight allotment go way up but I also had a mountain of mulch in my driveway chipped from the tree the city took down.

These chips would help me eradicate the lawn. After Sam convinced Louis that he wasn't going to be kicking a soccer ball around at this late date in his life, I convinced Louis the lawn could go. I covered the insidious Bermuda grass with flattened cardboard boxes and then topped that with a foot of the mulch. If I kept the mulch topped up as it decomposed, the grass would rot underneath and I would be free of the pernicious stuff.

Now that I had gotten rid of a few trees and the lawn, it was time to start deciding where to plant.

The trouble was, the soil in my yard was particularly dense clay. In some places the clay seemed to have been amended with plaster of paris, the dirt as hard and as fertile as concrete. I figured the best way to grow vegetables in such situations was in raised beds. I could put good soil in the beds and grow vegetables in places that were once only fit for parking the (now unnecessary) lawn mower.

A friend of mine gave me some heavy wooden beds that I used in one section of the back yard, but I needed more, and they needed to fit within some rather strangely shaped spaces—between those nonnegotiable patios and trees for instance. I also knew that come next year, or even next season, I might want to move the beds in order to rotate my crops or take advantage of (in the case of winter crops) the shifting light that would be available underneath trees that had lost their autumn leaves.

I could have planted in plastic burlap bags, and had done so before. While that worked okay, they didn't look very pretty, and I didn't like that when the bags weathered into trash within the year, I was throwing something else into the landfill. I needed raised beds that would be mobile, flexible, everlasting and inexpensive, and that wouldn't "reduce the aesthetic appearance of the neighborhood."

Paving stones turned out to be the answer.

My son Jesse, who had his own apartment on the other side of town, showed up to help with the beds. It wasn't too long ago that he would have rather cut off a thumb than do yard chores for his mom; but in a gratifying twist, the adolescent Jesse, so thin and pale we called him the translucent child, had grown up to become a gardening-loving Jesse and was strong as a horse to boot.

Our stones were eighteen-by-eighteen-inch brick-colored concrete, so Jesse dug a trench six to seven inches deep, placed the pavers on their sides to form the walls of the beds, and then set them with dirt. Completing the raised bed, we pounded the outside dirt with the flat end of the fifty-pound pry bar (I call it "the big nail") to keep them in place. The dirt inside the bed kept the stones from tipping inward.

I pointed to where I wanted the other beds to go, and in no time Jesse had worked raised-bed miracles. I was ready for dirt.

Green Food

When I was twelve, I made a devil's food cake and used green food coloring in the batter instead of red. I topped it off with chartreuse frosting.

I thought my brilliant-green triple-layer cake was spectacular. My father, however, wouldn't even try it. He said that food needed to *look* edible as well as taste good for him to eat it, and apparently, a goo-covered green tower didn't do it for him.

When it came to food, my father was a particular man, not only about the kind of meals he was served, but also about how much food the family ate. At least within sight of our parents, we kids did not eat more than two cookies at any one time. Seconds were frowned upon.

When my father refused to eat the cake, my mother must have figured wastefulness was worse than gluttony and told us kids we could eat it instead.

The whole cake. *All* of it. *At one time.*

I still feel a tinge of euphoria when I think of my sister and brother and me tucking into that green devil's food. I credit that experience for my certainty that experimentation makes cooking worthwhile. And that's what many of the "farmer recipes" in this book are—somewhat experimental—because their genesis depends on what is growing in the Quarter Acre Farm.

Every day, I go into the yard to pick and plan dinner (I admit to a perverse pleasure announcing at each meal where and when the main ingredient of the entree met its doom. I spear a tomato, and holding it aloft, say something ghoulish like, "*This* was still alive in the side yard while Dad was setting the table!" Louis and Sam roll their eyes). Our meal hinges on whatever ingredients I find ripe and ready. Therefore the recipes change every time I use them because the available ingredients differ every time I cook.

So, my green-chile chili is sometimes made with green chiles, but sometimes with red chiles, or with cranberry beans instead of pinto beans, or with more onion or less. Tomato soup can be tomato-zucchini soup if there aren't enough tomatoes, or tomato green-chile soup, or potato-tomato soup or tomato-apricot chutney soup, for that matter. The point is using what tastes good together or even *looks* good together. And luckily for a farmer, I think brilliant green is gorgeous . . . even in a cake.

DOLLAR FOR DIRT

*"To be a successful farmer one must
first know the nature of the soil"*
—EXNOPHON, OECONOMICUS, 400 B.C.

Our rabbit, Kwan Yin, is extremely friendly, which isn't a surprise given that Jesse toted her around in a baby pack for six months. Every girl in visual range would descend upon Jesse and Kwan Yin, cooing and petting her, which I believe was Jesse's intent. When Jesse developed an allergy to rabbits, or perhaps to rabbit *care*, Kwan Yin's days of living the life of a bunny pasha were over. She now lives in a pen in our yard along with Hestia, a companion rabbit we purchased solely to ease Kwan Yin's feelings of abandonment.

Some people think of rabbits as pets, some as a future meal. Some think they're both. It is a good thing rabbits are unaware of the dangerous borderland they inhabit. Imagine if every time someone stroked your hair you wondered if she was loving you or plotting to make stew and line her mittens with your pelt.

My mother once served us kids a rabbit we were fond of—in the guise of chicken. Our bellies full, she sprung the truth on us. It was like being told we'd eaten our Siamese cat, battered and fried. Worse, we'd really enjoyed it.

While Hestia and Kwan Yin are safe from our appetites, they are not strictly pets. When people ask if we plan to eat our rabbits, I tell them that just as knowing how to fish is a richer gift than a fish, there is something richer than a meal of rabbit. A fishing rabbit, certainly, but in lieu of that, a pooping one.

I believe that because I have come to understand the importance of dirt. In the past I figured that while good dirt was better than bad dirt, if a plant had enough water and sunshine it would grow just fine even if it were in sand. After all, look at hydroponics.

Of course, there is more to hydroponics than water, just as there is more to dirt than meets the eye. What is in dirt makes a difference not only to how robustly your crop grows, but also to how it tastes.

I knew a guy who raised a pig for meat on a little piece of property outside of Casper, Wyoming. The guy had a connection with a bakery wholesaler and got their expired cakes and cookies for free, so he fattened his pig on desserts. When the time came for the pig to be butchered, the meat from the porker was so sweet it was inedible. If there's a pig heaven, I'm sure the pig is pleased.

A study by Laura Parker, an agricultural activist in Northern California, showed that the dirt a pig grew up on, and on which grew the food the pig ate, had strong kinships to the flavor of its meat. In fact, a group of tasters could match the meat of the pig to the dirt it was raised on by sniffing various muds from both the pig's home and other places.

If dirt can flavor a pig through the eating of greens (or Twinkies), imagine what great dirt does to the flavor of the *greens*. I know that bad dirt can kill them entirely.

When I started my year of living off the Quarter Acre Farm, I purchased a mound of soil to fill some of the new raised beds. The soil was heavy, sandy, and closer to beige in color than umber. I filled several raised beds with the stuff and put in my plants. I also started my potatoes in bags using that dirt. The top of the dirt crusted after I watered it, and water ran off or pooled with each subsequent watering. When the dirt finally did absorb water, it became sodden. My potatoes rotted, seeds struggled to break through the crust, the nascent beets didn't have a chance, and the beans were malnourished.

Good dirt should have substance while still being fluffy. If you compress a damp handful in your fist, it should retain its shape when you loosen your grip, but just barely. It should be dark in color. It should smell good.

We no longer buy dirt, but make it ourselves, and rabbit manure is an important ingredient in our soil recipe.

Rabbit scat is wonder manure, higher in nitrogen than any other manure, with lots of phosphorus to aid in flower and fruit growth, and potassium for overall plant health. Further, it comes in small dry pellets (some call them bunny berries). It doesn't smell and it's filled with a good amount of organic matter. Because of this, the manure is not only feeding the plants but also building the soil.

Further still, a rabbit is productive. For every two tons of dry manure a steer produces a year, a relatively tiny rabbit produces one ton. (Which is why if you can find a rabbit farm raising the critters for pets, food, or fur, they are likely to be more than happy to provide you, gratis, with as many rabbit droppings as you are willing to cart away.) And while you must age steer manure, a rabbit's manure is "mild" enough that you can apply the stuff directly onto your growing beds. In fact, one can raise earthworms directly under the rabbit hutch. The worms eat the manure and produce castings, which is actually the worm's manure, which makes it manure squared. All of it is great for the garden.

Rabbit manure and worm castings are not the only ingredients of our soil recipe. We also collect leaves. Our neighbors have an enormous tree that in the spring and summer provides a small planet's worth of shade. In the fall the tree releases an impressive number of plate-sized leaves. The neighbors rake them up and put them neatly in the street for collection. I sneak out and take bunches of them to put in the leaf-mold pile.

I also add leaves to the compost. They are a high-carbon element and offset the high nitrogen component in the bin. For our purposes, it works to think of this as "dry fluffy" offsetting the "heavy smelly." They are also a good mulch for the garden, holding in moisture and smothering weeds. If you've got extra energy, you can shred the leaves to help them break down faster and to allow air and water to percolate through them in the beds.

I don't shred because I don't have extra energy. However, I've heard of some fun ways to do it. One guy shredded his leaves by putting them in windrows in the street and running his mower over them. Someone suggested putting leaves in a garbage can and running a string trimmer in it, much like lowering a hand mixer into chunky soup to make puree. I, boringly, but without using petroleum products, pile the leaves and bide my time until the leaf pile has become crumbly black and smells like rain.

We also collect coffee grounds for our dirt making. The coffee house a few blocks from the Quarter Acre Farm puts its (voluminous amounts of) used grounds in bags and gives them to customers. It is a happy day when I manage to lug four bags of coffee grounds to my bicycle, and even better when Louis is there with me and I can compel him to carry them home.

Coffee grounds are in high demand in the spring when thoughts turn to gardening. For a few months I'd see a guy I'll call "Joe" trying to score coffee grounds; sometimes I'd get them first, sometimes Joe would. I figured we had gardening in common, and I'd often try to start up a conversation as we sprinted for the grounds. But he must have thought I was trying to divert him from his quest, because Joe didn't just ignore me, he glared. Compost is serious business. Louis said maybe it was more than serious; maybe Joe was using the coffee to mask the odor of a dead body. It was more likely he was masking the odor of his compost.

The last ingredient of Quarter Acre Farm dirt is kitchen refuse. We collect all peels, trimmings, and old fruits and vegetables in a mini garbage can on the kitchen counter. I used to be more open about my avid composting, and our neighbors would bring us their watermelon rinds to compost, but then an acquaintance showed up at my door one day and presented me with a large black Hefty sack ballooning with gasses from the decomposition of fermenting vegetable muck. Confusing the horror on my face with awe, she assured me she would bring more next month. I managed to thank her but told her I had more than I could handle, actually.

Ick. I had changed my own babies' dirty diapers with no problem but gagged at any other child's. Now I knew I only had tolerance for my own family's compost as well.

When our mini kitchen garden can was full, or when it emitted a cloud of stink when we cracked the lid, we emptied it into the larger bin in the yard. Our outdoor compost bin, which we got as part of a city composting project, is a black plastic box about the size of one of those ubiquitous, neon-colored, plastic playhouses for children. We dump not only the kitchen compost into the outside bin, but also the plant trimmings and bedding from the goose kennel. We do nothing more with it, but you could turn it every week for faster results. Some say you should turn it—some say it vehemently. I'll say it again: composting is serious business. The most impolite exchanges I have ever read on blog threads between gardeners deal with compost and whether to turn or not to turn—and it all hinges on bacteria.

Thonius Philips van Leeuwenhoek is to blame. He was a Renaissance kind of guy two hundred years after the Renaissance was over. He owned the largest drapery business in the Dutch town of Delft and used very basic microscopes to look at the details of cloth. He also made over five hundred microscopes himself and used them to look at and describe what he called "animalcules," or amoebas (thereby becoming the "father of microbiology"), and what we would eventually call bacteria. How does he tie in with compost?

Organic matter breaks down in nature owing largely to the work of fungi and bacteria. Some of those bacteria function best at middle temperatures (mesophylic) and others at high temperatures (thermophylic). Turning the compost introduces oxygen into the pile, which the aerobic bacteria like. The mesophylic bacteria create heat as they do their bacterial work, which raises the temperature inside the compost to the point the thermophylic fellas begin to thrive. Like the friend with the outrageously high metabolism who gets twenty times more done than middling me, the higher temp bacteria work faster than the middle temperature ones. Therefore turning makes for faster compost.

However, there are those who say turning the compost mixes up the thermophylically active layers of compost with those layers that are already "done," actually *hindering* the thermophylic work and messing up the lower layers of composted material for things like earthworms and the aforementioned fungi, which not only break down the tougher material in nature but also further improve the soil.

What would Thonius say? He is safely out of the picture, leaving us to decide what we will. I won't weigh in on the science of it. I am lazy, so I simply don't turn our compost. After dumping the scraps in the composter, we layer leaves or straw or coffee on top of the scraps. This layering seems to keep our system pretty balanced and sweet smelling, and the coffee helps deter pests like raccoons, possums, and rats.

However, we still get a few pests. Our cat, Tiger, thinks the rats he catches and places in my path so that I step barefoot on their plump bodies are fine by-products of composting. Once, Jesse was in the backyard by the composter at dusk and reached out and petted our white cat, Orion, as she walked along the fence. "Orion" hissed at him and bared a row of dagger-sharp teeth. Jesse is the only person I know who has ever scratched an opossum behind the ears. Experiences like that have made us much more attentive recyclers, especially making sure that no rodent-tempting dairy and meat products find their way into our pile.

When I find myself in need of dirt, I go to the composter, fork the barely composted stuff and the semi-composted stuff to the side (this is the one time the newer layers do get "turned"), then dig out the pretty well composted stuff and put it in a wheelbarrow. To the barrow I add leaf mold, rabbit manure, and more used coffee grounds. If the mixture seems too heavy, I fork in some straw or dry leaves to fluff it up. (Note: Do not use hay . . . straw is the dry stems of wheat generally used for bedding. Hay is grass, used to feed animals, replete with seeds, which will sprout in your beds and require more weeding, which nobody needs.) This makes lovely, dark, rich dirt, with the occasional uncomposted eggshell or orange peel thrown in. I consider this a mark of authenticity, much as the odd smirch in a glaze adds to a vase's beauty. As my old pottery instructor used to say, "If you want perfect, go to Kmart."

Making dirt isn't as easy as having dirt dumped into the driveway, but it's worth it. As they say, a dollar for dirt, a penny for seeds. Especially if you are somewhat of a bumbler like me—forgetting to water or watering too much, unsure what fertilizer to use and how much, growing plants in not quite the right spot, and planting too early or too late in the season—then starting off with good, rich, sweet dirt will make the greatest difference in ameliorating your not-so-green thumb.

Beet and Chevre Sandwiches

had never tasted a fresh beet until my year of living off the Quarter Acre Farm. That first beet wasn't even one I had grown. My friend John showed up one day with a warty-looking vegetable the size of a softball and gave it to me. I thanked him doubtfully then asked what I was supposed to do with it. He told me to boil it.

I didn't want to throw a gift away, so I trimmed the greens, stuck the gnarly thing into a pot of simmering water for about twenty minutes, then let it cool.

It still didn't look like anything I'd be willing to put in my mouth. But when I picked it up to peel it, the skin slipped off like a glove. It was like a fairytale, but instead of the toad turning into a hunky prince, the crepuscular root suddenly shone like sunshine. I think I said, "Wow."

Since then I've grown lots of beets. I love red beets but my favorite is still the golden beet. I don't care for chioggas. Though their concentric red and white rings look impressive, they taste soapy to me. I've heard this is a genetic marker, like being able to roll your tongue.

One of the many ways I eat beets is in sandwiches. I especially like them in sourdough panini with goat cheese. Both the sour bread and the tart cheese highlight the sweetness of the beets, while the crusty bread and greens give a crunchy counterpoint to the tender beets and the creamy chevre.

Here's what you need:
- Several small to medium beets—red, golden, or chiogga
- A loaf of crusty sourdough bread
- Goat cheese
- Balsamic vinegar and olive oil

Cut the beet leaves from the beetroot about an inch from the crown, making sure you don't cut into the beet itself. Set aside the most tender beet greens. Gently boil the whole beets for 15 to 30 minutes until a fork pierces the root easily (or roast them at 425 degrees for 30 to 45 minutes until they are fork tender).

When they've cooled, the skins will slip off easily. Dice the cooled beet, cut the tender beet greens into chiffonade, then combine and toss the mixture with a splash of balsamic vinegar and olive oil.

Spread a thick layer of goat cheese between two pieces of bread and grill on the panini press. When the sandwich is hot, remove to a plate, open the sandwich, and spoon the beet mixture on top of the cheese. Season with salt and pepper and place the second piece of bread back on top—or spoon the beet mixture on both halves of the sandwich and serve open-faced.

TOFU OF THE WEST

"Zucchini's terrific! Like bunnies prolific!"
—AUTHOR UNKNOWN

By late July my zucchini had been productive for some time. Good thing, because the rest of the garden was not exactly living up to my Edenesque expectations—the cucumbers were ratty, the beans slow, and the tomato production practically nonexistent. But I could count on the zucchini. I weighed out, ate, and logged into my book what seemed like truckloads of zukes in just the first month.

Though I was eating tons of this cucumber-shaped summer squash, I was a little desperate for variety, and that made me cranky and territorial. If I saw Sam with a handful of cherry tomatoes I'd snap, "Where did you get those?" Louis with a plum in hand was subjected to interrogation as well. "Is that mine? Are you sure? Which bowl did you get it out of?" If they wouldn't take part in the Quarter Acre Farm experiment, they could get their food elsewhere.

Of course, that was fine with them. They'd noticed me gnawing on grilled zucchini day in and day out. I ate grilled zucchini on couscous and grilled zucchini on rice, grilled zucchini with chutney, and grilled zucchini alongside more grilled zucchini. Louis and Sam looked on, certain that they had called this experiment correctly, all the more thrilled with their pork chops.

But as I approached August, my questionable good fortune of having endless zucchini was threatened. Suddenly the zucchini didn't look so good either.

For one thing, the plant had writhed its way onto the pathway. Anyone walking through the garden risked becoming entangled and falling into the abyss of leaves—leaves that made it increasingly difficult to find the vegetables until they were of human scale. (Sam and I found a zucchini so large that we poked holes in it and stuck candles all along the limb-like vegetable. We had a unique candelabra for months—until we noticed a puddle of squash rot seeping along the dining room table.)

The humans and cats that thrashed their way through the zucchini roadblock eventually left the leaves looking battered. The leaves began turning yellow, were oddly fuzzy, and definitely brittle. Whether it was in protest of being stepped on, exhaustion from having formed too many monster-sized zucchini, or the result of disease that seemed to be galloping through the plant, my zucchini's fruit production slowed considerably.

About the time things were looking their worst, a gardening friend said she was stopping by to see the Quarter Acre Farm. Staring at the mess of unsightly vegetation, I decided no leaves would look better than sick leaves, so I trimmed every yellow, brown, and battered leaf off both my zucchini and my cucumber plants. Once I started trimming, I noticed that my bush-type zucchini plants weren't really bushes. They were vines off of which leaves bushily sprouted. Once noted, I gently coiled the thick stems into a loose circle, much as one would coil a hose or a rope. It worked like a charm. No longer did the zucchini run amok; instead they grew happily 'round in about a three-by-three-foot space.

The shorn vines *did* look better for the visit, but the astonishing thing to me was how in the days to come, the trimming gave my zucchini and cucumber plants a new lease on life. The new leaves remained healthy longer, and plants started producing loads of fruit once again.

I suppose it shouldn't have hit me as such a miraculous cure. Squash leaves are prone to all sorts of bacterial and fungal diseases, including scab infections, leaf spot, leaf blot, and downy mildew. Trimming away a diseased or infested leaf is going to help keep the problem from migrating to other leaves. It allows for better air circulation through the plant, which also helps curb disease. Finally, trimming a dying leaf frees the plant from supporting foliage that is not likely to be doing much photosynthesis at that point anyway.

The zucchini began to produce so prolifically that I rescinded my moratorium on Louis and Sam eating food from the garden—zucchini at least. But Louis and Sam said they were already sick of grilled zucchini, just having watched me eat so much of it. If I wanted them to eat zucchini, I would have to expand my repertoire of zucchini culinaria.

I began asking around, and it was as if zucchini recipes were genetically programmed into humans: the breadth of variety was amazing.

In painting parlance, pigments are carried by what is known as a "vehicle"—oil paints are pigments carried by the vehicle linseed oil, acrylics are pigments carried by a polymer vehicle, encaustic's vehicle is wax.

Zucchini is a cooking vehicle. Possessed of mild taste and texture, it carried whatever flavors I gave it. It was the tofu of the western world.

A wealth of zucchini recipes at my disposal, I sautéed zucchini with garlic and red pepper and served it over pasta. I stuffed it with breadcrumbs, egg, tomatoes, and spices. I stir fried it and made a zucchini curry. I used my mandolin and cut it into long, fine. julienned "noodles" and tossed it with olive oil and shredded Parmesan.

I baked little pizza crusts made out of shredded zucchini, egg, and flour, and topped them with tomato and cheese. I stirred up sloppy zucchini joes, panko-crusted zucchini crisps, zucchini filo tart. Zucchini carried the day in soup, quiche, frittata, fritters with fig, cold zucchini spring rolls, zucchini lasagna with zucchini-tomato-eggplant pasta sauce, savory zucchini bread, zucchini parmigiana, zucchini with quinoa, and of course, ratatouille.

I also made several kinds of sweet zucchini breads, the best being sweetened with fig and homemade plum butter.

As I delved deeper into the zucchini's culinary possibilities, I found it wasn't only the zucchini fruit that was edible. Zucchini was one of those foods that lent itself to a kind of eating the Italians refer to as *cucina di recupero,* or "recovery food," in which nothing of a plant goes to waste. You can eat all parts of the zucchini plant, including the leaves. I like them deep fried, and I also blanch them and use them like grape leaves to roll rice or meat within.

Zucchini flowers, which are difficult not to anthropomorphize, are either male (the flower is larger and on a long stem), or female (the flower is attached to a small round fruit that swells into voluptuousness during the life of the zucchini). The cadmium-colored flowers can be left on the tiny zucchini and the fruit and flower sautéed together, or the flower can be separated from the fruit, chopped, and used in quesadillas or soups, stirred into frittatas, or sprinkled onto salads. I pinched the sepals off the whole flowers and stuffed the delicate blossoms with cheeses and fish, then steamed, sautéed, or fried them.

Except for the night of the disgusting panko-crusted crisps, which weren't crisp at all but resembled snot, and the savory zucchini bread that chewed like a slice of parmesan-flecked bike tire, the weeks of zucchini dinners weren't a nightmare, but ranged from pretty good to out-and-out great, if I do say so myself. Sam and Louis even ate the zucchini meals with me.

In spite of our daily consumption, I still had excess zucchini. Luckily I found zucchini is a snap to save for later. You don't have to peel zucchini; in fact, you shouldn't peel it, as the skins are the most nutritious part—a good source of thiamin, niacin, vitamins A, C, and B6, phosphorus, and manganese. The seeds are soft, edible, and full of fiber.

I cut the zucchini into one-eighth-inch-thick rounds and put them in the dehydrator to dry, or placed the rounds in a single layer on a cookie sheet and froze them. They required no blanching, no dipping in lemon to retain their color, nothing fancy. Once frozen, I packed the zucchini circles into freezer bags so I could grab a handful to use in soups, lasagnas, and stews.

I also grated the zucchini, especially the big ones (which had proportionally larger seeds so I halved them lengthwise and scooped out the seeds, giving them a miniature canoe look). I put two cups of the grated zucchini in the potato ricer, squeezed the excess water out, and then plonked what I called the "zucchini puck" onto a cookie sheet. After I had a number of the two-cup pucks, I packed them in bags and froze them.

In the fall and winter, when the wide leaves of my zucchini plants were all but memories, I could still enjoy the squash. I pulled my pucks of zucchini from the freezer and stirred up some zucchini fritters, or I sautéed zucchini with tomatoes and a hot chili pepper and pureed it into soup.

At this point I was ready to nominate zucchini as vegetable of the year. Reading up on my new favorite vegetable, I decided we should go a step further and change the phrase "American as apple pie" to "American as zucchini bread." Neither apples nor apple pie are indigenous to the Americas (think *apfelstrudel* and tarte tatin), but both zucchini and zucchini bread are.

All squash are American natives, but the zucchini went to Europe a bitter-fleshed pepo gourd and came back the sweet courgette we know and love. This was not the result of an expensive finishing school, as the courgette's name would imply, but of a spontaneously occurring mutation called a "sport" or bud variation, the kind that spurred the grapefruit from the pumelo, the pink grapefruit from the grapefruit, and the brussels sprout from the common heading cabbage.

Adding to zucchini's American nativity is the fact that Thomas Jefferson himself issued the very first U.S. patent for the other crucial element to zucchini bread: baking soda, or at least the precursor to baking soda, pearlash. It is likely that zucchini and pearlash came together in the eighteenth century to become zucchini bread when housewives in America discovered pearlash as a chemical leavening. The chemical reaction of alkaline pearlash mixed with a clabber, such as buttermilk, introduced bubbles into the dough, creating a lighter biscuit. What innovation! How much more patriotic can it get?

If zucchini bread was named our national dish, then August 8 could be "Leave Zucchini on Your Neighbor's Porch Day"—a national holiday rather than a gardener's prank. (Why do people in *fill in your state here* lock their cars in the summer? To keep them from being filled with zucchini!) This would give August, a month bereft of holidays, a day of celebration.

That might have been my last word on the wonders of zucchini, but as an unanticipated perk, in the first two months of eating so much zucchini through July and August, I lost ten pounds. Losing ten pounds is not easy for me. In fact, I've turned over the idea of offering my body to science to facilitate the study of persistent hips. Suddenly though, and with no effort, I became practically lean. Once again I was surprised by the unsurprising—eating fruits and vegetables as 75 percent of my diet was healthy in many ways.

Louis wasn't so sure. He feared I would whittle down to nothing. To allay his fears I went to my doctor for a consultation. I sheepishly explained that I was taking her time away from the truly sick and injured patients because I had hit my ideal weight and felt great. As she checked me over, I explained to her what I was doing on the Quarter Acre Farm.

Somewhat quizzically, she congratulated me on my health as she went out the door to deal with someone who truly needed her.

Since I'd found yet another reason to celebrate the lofty zucchini squash, I decided to plant even more zucchini the following season. It occurred to me, however, that if the popularity of zucchini grew, it could actually crush the holiday it's named after. For once discovering the wonder of zucchini, who in their right minds would give the magic vegetables away? Perhaps on August 8, we might instead leave seeds on our neighbor's porch, or collections of recipes. And maybe every so often, just because they're so awe-inspiring, a giant zucchini candelabra.

Grilled Zucchini

This is my go-to recipe. One that allowed me to remain well fed and among the living while waiting for the other plants on the farm to start producing. The recipe is easy and good enough to eat several nights a week, though every single day for a month may be pushing it.

I use as many zucchini as I'm hungry for and use any size available. If I've got zucchini coming out my ears, I try to harvest them while small, with the blossoms still attached, and grill them halved lengthwise. If the zucchini are on the other end of the spectrum, really big guys, I cut out the seeds so that just the firm flesh and the green skin are left.

Ingredients:
- 8 six-inch zucchini
- 2 TB honey
- 1 TB olive oil
- 1 TB finely minced rosemary
- 1 TB finely minced orange peel
- ⅛ tsp cayenne pepper
- salt to taste

Cut the zucchini into pieces 3 to 4 inches long and about the girth of your thumb, making sure each has a side with green skin.

Place the trimmed zucchini into a big bowl, drizzle with honey and olive oil, and then scatter the finely minced rosemary, orange peel, and cayenne pepper over that. Stir until an even coat of the seasonings adhere to the surface of the zucchini. (This is why you must *finely* mince the rosemary and orange peel. Too-large pieces will not stick.)

When I'm doing this at home, I heat my embarrassingly grungy-looking grill (it's *seasoned*) to medium-high heat in order to cook the outside of the zucchini fast while keeping the inside a little crispy. I put the sticky zucchini on the grill until they get a nice brown color on one side (merely heated is not good enough; they need to be brown—it is this caramelization that makes the zucchini so good). Using tongs, I turn them over and sear the other side, and then remove the zukes to a plate. The rosemary and citrus notes of this lightly spiced grilled zucchini is lovely and makes this dish great as a side— even if you don't want to eat them as your entire meal.

SADISM IN THE GARDEN

*"Most plants taste better when
they've had to suffer a little."*
—DIANE ACKERMAN

In a not-so-funny twist, while the zucchini *looked* bad but kept up production, my tomatoes *appeared* fantastic—the Chippendales of the garden, sporting strong limbs and good color, throwing blossoms left and right, and seemingly bursting with virility—but they were giving me *no* satisfaction. There was nary a tomato on most of the plants.

This was a matter of great embarrassment for me. Tomatoes are, of course, the reason to garden. Even my gardening-phobic friend tries, every other year, to grow her own tomatoes. Tomatoes are the most common homegrown vegetable in the nation.

To make the humiliation worse, the area where I live is not only the tomato capital of California but also a hotbed for the slow-food movement (whose members support the heritage, tradition, and culture of food that is good for the people who eat it and for the people who grow it, while being good for the planet.) These two facts pull the local tomato-growing population in differing directions. Slow food people enjoy a tomato with a lumpy physique as long as it tastes great, while commercial growers, on

the other hand, would love to have the best tasting tomato in the world but often have to sacrifice this for profitability. They need to grow large quantities of tomatoes in uniform shapes and sizes that fit into boxes, are tough enough to ship well, and still look good displayed in the grocery store—if some taste must be sacrificed, so be it. The former faction prefers heirlooms and the latter hybrids.

I knew what kind of farmer I was going to be. I was eschewing pesticides and herbicides and living the organic life—I was going for the heirlooms.

The trouble is, growing any kind of tomato isn't as easy as it would seem, despite evidence to the contrary: the vast fields of tomatoes around my town and the mountains of knobby, striped, spotted heirlooms gracing the aisles of the farmer's market, with romantic names like Arkansas Traveler, Aunt Ruby's German Green, and Noir de Crème. No, growing tomatoes can be downright difficult.

By the time I had decided to live off my quarter acre, I had already grown lots of tomatoes over the years. Or at least *some* tomatoes on a lot of tomato plants. I even remember my mother growing tomatoes back when I was a kid and thought heirlooms were cracked dishes and tarnished silver. She would plant her tomatoes in June then pull the plants in early September to protect them from frost. She'd hang the plants by their roots in the basement hoping some of the immature tomatoes would ripen. The acrid green smell would rise along the concrete walls and make my mouth water.

Relocating from Wyoming to California had extended my tomato-growing season a great deal. But even with an extra four months of growing time, my plants never produced enough tomatoes to make a winter's worth of spaghetti sauce, soup, and sun-dried tomatoes.

With the Quarter-Acre Farm project, however, I planned to leave mediocrity behind and become a great tomato farmer. I planted several different kinds of heirlooms and then read everything I could on how to raise them.

I searched the Internet for tomato advice until my eyes felt like they'd been sandpapered. I asked friends, family, and neighbors for tomato secrets. I was laved with advice. The trouble was that some of it was *non-advice,* the equivalent of a recipe with an ingredient missing, "I just pop them in and they grow!" Or sometimes the advice I got from one source seriously conflicted with the advice from another. And each expert was so *certain.*

The flowers would fail to set fruit, I read, because they got too much water. Another source claimed it was more likely there wasn't enough water. If the days were too hot, the plants would fail to produce, but they'd also fail if it was too cold. When I rode my bike around the tomato fields, I could see that the commercial growers let their tomatoes grow with the vines slumped onto the dirt, though I had just heard *that* was a definite no-no. Some people let their tomato's foliage grow rampant to encourage photosynthesis, while others trimmed flowerless branches (or "widows," as my friend Emily called them) to allow better circulation, or to ensure energy would go to the fruit rather than the leaves.

It seemed that every gardener had her own particular tomato theory, which I allowed made sense. Each gardener, after all, had their own particular garden, their own types of plants, soil, climate, air, and light conditions. It was not only true that what worked for a gardener in California was not going to work for my mother in Wyoming, but also, clearly, that what worked for someone on the north side of town may not work for someone living on the south side.

In light of all this, and feeling a little like a flower child, I decided to let my tomatoes grow unpruned, unfettered, and free. This worked fine for weeks, and the plants grew bushy. But when I noticed that the sow bugs (which are so numerous on the Quarter-Acre Farm I've thought of trying to eat them and kill two birds with one stone) were, instead of me, freely enjoying the few tomatoes flopped on the ground, I knew I had to change my strategy.

I tied the prone plants up to some rickety cages I bought at the hardware store, but this helped only until the plants grew a little more, at which point the cages toppled over. I tried several different methods of support, including rolled construction fencing, which I didn't notice had holes too small for me to stick my hand through until it was too late. For me to reach the tomatoes, Louis had to cut bigger holes in it using wire snips.

I also tied tomatoes up to peeler poles pounded into the ground. This worked quite well but was a little messy because the plants had to curve around the single pole, and searching for tomatoes in the resulting riot of foliage was difficult. Also, the poles had a tendency to rot in the damp ground. After the first season, the eight-foot poles only had five useful feet to them.

I found my ideal support in four-feet-high by eight-feet-long galvanized steel wire panels, which have a smaller grid (2" x 4") toward the bottom and a larger grid (4" x 4") at the top. I could get a twenty-by four-foot livestock panel for thirty dollars and grow a row of plants along it. These panels are virtually indestructible, look good, store easily, and work great for growing peas, beans, squash, and melons as well.

As my tomatoes grew tall and verdant, I thrilled. When all the flowers fell off, I panicked. I thought perhaps my plants were in need of more fertilizer; after all, isn't food always welcome in times of stress? When the fertilizing didn't help, I did a little research and found I had done exactly the wrong thing. When soil temperatures rise, the tomato plant drives its roots deeper into the cool earth. Adding fertilizer forces plants into a foliage growth mode when it should be focusing on getting its roots to a cool spot instead. What I could have done to help the plant to that end was mulch. Three to four inches of mulch can keep the soil five degrees cooler and the plant producing tomatoes.

So I mulched. My plants *still* dropped flowers. I decided to take a trip over to see my friends, Alan and Emily, and get some advice. Their tomato plants looked great and had lots of fruit hanging on the *pruned* vines. Maybe, I mused, tomatoes were like children and needed boundaries rather than complete freedom. I described my tomatoes and growing process to Alan (the tomato guru). He thought I might be watering my plants too much. When I wailed, "How can anyone tell what the right amount is?" He said, "You let them suffer. Hold off on the water until they just start to wilt—and *then* you save them. Suffer and save."

Quite an uncivil attitude, especially from my kindly friend Alan, but he loves tomatoes even more than I do, which is scary, and I was going to take his advice. By the time I had blundered through all this, however, it was getting late in the growing season. As it goes in the Central Valley, while the nighttime temps were cooling alarmingly fast, whispering in my ear with a chill breath, "You are going to be soooooo hungry in February," the daytime temperatures were still torrid.

The temperature change was also problem in tomato growing. Not only do heated soil conditions signal a tomato to stop producing, but chill soil temperatures do as well. Air temperatures above 85 degrees do the same. Further, hot-dry means difficulty in pollinating, and as a result, no fruit will set. So I got up early each morning, and whilst still in my ratty bathrobe, I flicked tomato blossoms, hoping to shake pollen from one important part of the flower to the other.

Feeling a bit like an S&M tomato pimp, I spent half an hour every day shaking the tomato plants down and thumping the heck out of the blossoms. I got a few more tomatoes as a result, but only on certain plants. I had to face the fact that I was, once again, a tomato dilettante—except, strangely enough, for my success with the cherry tomatoes.

I am not usually a cherry tomato fan. I figure why spend extra time picking twenty little tomatoes when you can pick one giant tomato instead? But before I had decided on the Quarter Acre Farm experiment, I had planted two plants, supposedly as a treat for Sam (though he was now prohibited from eating them.) These two plants provided me with a plethora of fruit.

Each day, I would pick the tomatoes straight into a Ziploc bag and toss them into the freezer. They froze beautifully into what looked and felt like gorgeous red marbles. When I wanted to make sauce or soup, I'd take the bag and pour the "marbles" into the saucepan or blender and cook them up. They were a lifesaver, preserving me from certain tomato sauce withdrawal during the winter months.

In November, the embarrassingly barren tomato plants shriveled and blackened from the cold and I pulled them from the beds. That's when I noticed the bumps on the roots. The usually thick straight roots off of which the fibrous lateral roots grew were distorted and studded with nodules, or knots. When I uprooted tomato after tomato I found that most of their roots had the same strange lumps. Rightly sensing these nodules might be a clue to the poor showing of my tomatoes, I took my sinking feeling inside to search for information. To my horror, I found the nodules were symptoms of nematodes.

Nematodes are the most numerous multicellular animals on the planet with over 20,000 species of the critters. All are structurally simple "worms." The best description I've found is that they are a tube (an alimentary canal extending from the mouth to the tail) within a tube.

All nematodes are not created equal. There are good nematodes and bad nematodes. Just as if they were characters in a fairy tale, the good ones are very good and will kill your dragons (or at least cutworms) for you, and the bad ones have black hats, fetid breath, and lay waste to the kingdom. Actually, it isn't their breath that is a problem, it's their destructive saliva. The bad nematodes burrow into the roots and inject their saliva into the plant to fashion feeding cells. Not only does this residence restrict the ability of the roots to conduct water and nutrients (kind of like parking a Volkswagen in a water pipe), but the galls can split and allow soilborne disease-causing microorganisms into the plant. The next thing you know, your tomato plant has bacterial spot, speck, canker, wilt, pith necrosis; or loses vigor, yellows, and produces smaller and fewer fruits while everyone else has bragging rights to Cherokee Purples the size of bread loaves.

I was stricken. It was like finding out my garden had cancer. Indeed, the "cure" for nematodes is elusive. One hopes only to manage them. Large farms that have a nematode infestation allow acres to sit stripped and fallow so the nematodes starve, dry out, and die. Fallowing and soil solarization, even if one was willing to let everything in their garden die for a year, generally only reduces the nematodes in the top foot of the soil, and worse, is effective for only about a year.

Louis, Sam, and Jesse tried to comfort me as I faced a future without homegrown tomatoes. I resisted their cajoling, knowing it was only a matter of time before my yard would be a desolate plat of shriveled plants, my Quarter Acre Farm experiment a total bust. After a few days of moping, I stiffened my wobbly spine and did still more research. I eventually found that ammonia and nitrogen-rich fertilizers might depress nematode growth. Well, the ducks, chickens, and geese were doing their parts there. I also learned that certain plants had a tendency to repel nematodes with antagonistic phytochemical exudates. Phew. This meant that plants like the French Single Gold marigold, Burpee's nemagold, and blanket flowers make stuff that protects them against the worms, much like flavenoids and lycopene protect us against cancer. I put marigolds on my to-buy list.

Chitin, too, depresses nematode numbers because fungi that eat chitin also eat nematode eggs. You could get that at a gardener's supply shop along with red plastic sheeting to lay over the planting surface. Red plastic doubles nematode-infected tomato yields by reflecting light, which encourages above-ground growth over root growth, making the plants less susceptible to soilborne infection and infestation.

I was already feeling much better about my garden's future when I ran across a list of nematode-resistant tomatoes. I jotted down the names, including Park's Whopper Improved, Better Boy, Beefmaster, Miracle Sweet, and Celebrity. I had grown many of these in the past and had, now understandably, much better success with them than other cultivars. The cherry tomatoes I had planted had been (luckily) a type of nematode resistant hybrid.

Apparently I would have to remove the green H for Heirloom from my breast and replace it with the scarlet H for Hybrid and plant all resistant breeds from now on. At least until a nematode resistant heirloom made itself apparent.

I felt bad about this but for two things. One, the relief that I was going to be able to grow tomatoes at all; and two, because of an article by agricultural scientist Brendan Borrell stating that heirloom tomatoes are feeble, inbred products of centuries worth of breeding experiments.

It wasn't that I felt heirloom tomatoes were the sinus-challenged pugs of the tomato world. What gave me solace was Borrell's claim that heirlooms tasted good *not* because of genetics, but because they were ripened on the vine and their lower numbers of fruit per plant made for a juicier, tastier product.

It was the nurture, he was saying, that made the difference. And certainly, if I couldn't plant heirloom tomatoes, I could treat the tomatoes I did plant with the same care. Though I was quite certain that the taste of certain heirlooms was not entirely nurture, at least I knew now that all was not lost for the Quarter-Acre Farm.

The following spring, invigorated by a winter's worth of anticipation and planning, I planted again, mulching with red plastic. My tomato starts, all nematode-resistant varieties, went in on April 1, the day Alan recommended. I hoped this would give the plants enough time to establish and set fruit before the Central Valley's killer heat hit us in July and August (when I would apply several inches of mulch to keep the dirt temperature moderated). I followed the "suffer and save" watering dictum, and I became a pincher and a pruner to boot. (My plants were of the *indeterminate* variety that had no predisposed stopping point for their growth. *Determinate* tomatoes, which grow only to the point that a flower cluster forms at the terminal growth point, should *not* be pruned, because pruning curtails its fruit production.) I pinched off widows, and though my tomato plants didn't look very Chippendale pretty at first, I trimmed *all* foliage away, beginning from the ground and moving, twelve to eighteen inches up the main stem.

I was mean and heartless, whacking away foliage, forcing order, and withholding water. My tomatoes produced as though they thrived on nastiness. I finally had enough tomatoes to freeze, to dry, to render into quarts and quarts of sauce, and of course, to eat. In fact, I weighed most of that second summer's tomato crop and even without counting the volumes of tomatoes we ate standing in the garden, or the bowls of them we picked to give to neighbors and friends, my plants produced over *eight hundred pounds* of tomatoes. And they were delicious.

Roasted Tomato Sauce

This is the easiest, best recipe ever. Throw a mountain o' produce (it hardly matters which kinds or how many, just ensure a preponderance of tomatoes) into a roasting pan, toss the roasting pan into a roasting hot oven for a few hours, stir every twenty minutes, cool, then puree with a drizzle of olive oil and some salt and pepper. That's it.

This is the typical summer sauce scenario: I have picked a vast mountain of vegetables, most of which are tomatoes. Not only are these vegetables too numerous for our family to eat before they take a turn for the worse, but many of them are split or have bird pecks, strange shapes, or blossom scars that keep me from proudly gifting them to the neighbors. All of this goes into the sauce, which I make at least once a week through the last half of the summer, then freeze in one-meal servings. The ingredients vary wildly depending on what vegetables are in season, but I try to include vegetables from each of three categories:

- **Body vegetables**—tomatoes are the first and most important ingredient, making up at least half to three quarters of the total contents. Any combination of ripe surplus veggies can be used to fill out the rest, including eggplant, zucchini, beets, chard, and spinach.
- **Aromatic vegetables**—including onions, peppers (sweet and hot), garlic, and herbs.
- **Sweet produce**—to balance out the acidic tomatoes, I've used everything from carrots to figs, and even peaches.

The more tomatoes you use, the redder the sauce will be. A greater percentage of non-red vegetables makes for a browner-hued sauce. Of course, each batch tastes differently, sometimes just barely and sometimes considerably, such as when I use hot peppers rather than sweet peppers. But it is always good and always easy.

Additional Ingredients:
- 1 slosh olive oil
- salt and pepper to taste

1. After the sun has gone down and the world has cooled from torrid to merely beastly hot, and I can coax a breeze through the open windows, I set the oven to 475 degrees.

2. As the oven heats, I wash the vegetables, cut off the blemishes, and chop the bigger vegetables into halves or quarters (it is especially wise to do this with tomatoes to avoid having roasting tomato bombs explode on you when you stir your sauce mid-roast.)

3. I put these trimmed/chopped vegetables in the roasting pan and try to ensure that the more delicate vegetables, like the spinach and herbs, are buried under the bigger, wetter vegetables so they won't dry out and burn before the concoction has a chance to get good and sloppy.

4. I put the whole shebang in the hot oven, set the timer for thirty minutes, then go lay on the couch with the paper and the fan. Setting the timer is the most important direction in this recipe. It has been a long day and it is hot and therefore not inconceivable that a hardworking farmer might fall asleep while contemplating number seventeen across on the *New York Times* crossword puzzle.

5. When the timer sounds, I stir the pot, then set the timer again. I repeat the stirring and the setting until the vegetables look like glop. To get the vegetables to glop stage will take anywhere from two to four hours depending on the amount of vegetables you are roasting.

6. When it looks like glop, I turn off the oven, leaving the roasting pan in there, and then I go to bed.

7. When I wake up in the morning I use my crazy-powerful 1970s jet engine-loud Vita-Mix blender that can pulverize wood blocks into cream (when I use it, I wear hearing protectors and look like I work on a tarmac, albeit in a ratty bathrobe) and puree the sauce with a slosh of olive oil and a handful of basil leaves. If you don't have such a blender, you might want to pull the tomato skins from the glop before pureeing, or sieve the sauce afterward. For sauce the consistency of tomato paste, don't add water. For saucier sauce, add water—which has the added benefit of making the glop easier to puree.

8. Pour each blender batch of pureed sauce into a large bowl. When all has been pureed, stir to homogenize the flavors, add salt and pepper to taste, then ladle about three cup increments into freezer-safe bags or cups. Label with the dominant flavors ("tomato eggplant," or "tomato-zucchini-fig," or "spicy tomato hot-pepper") and freeze.

This is heavenly good tomato sauce. Heat and use the sauce for lasagna, in stews, over or in polenta, or as pizza sauce. Of course, this sauce is also great with pasta, as is.

SUGAR GROWS ON TREES

"A table, a chair, a bowl of fruit.
What else does a man need to be happy?"
—ALBERT EINSTEIN

If for some unfathomable reason, I was forced to eat an entire whale, I'd lie on the beach afterward, my stomach distended to the size of a Volkswagen, and I'd still ask, "Does anyone have a cookie?"

A meal needs something sweet at the end, *no matter what.* Jesse put it best when he was a little guy. Claiming to be too full to finish his dinner, he'd allow that he could, however, eat some cake. He explained that although the stomach itself could be absolutely stuffed, there is an anatomical dessert pocket alongside the stomach that's ever available for sweets.

Making sure my own dessert pocket is going to be filled is a constant preoccupation of mine, and I admit to eating a meal just to get to the sugary payoff at the end. Therefore I worried about how eating off the Quarter Acre Farm for a year would affect my predilection toward dessert. We had some fruit trees in the yard, and though they were young, I prayed they would provide enough of a fructose high to sate my voracious sweet tooth.

I haven't always thought of fruit as a dessert. When I was a kid complaining of being hungry my mother would say, "Eat a piece of fruit!" She might as well have directed us to eat tennis balls. The fruit I remember from my childhood was horrible. The name "red delicious" apple should have been "mushy tasteless" apple, without a doubt. Other fruit was no better: apricots were sour, oranges dry, and while half of the grapes in the bunch were firm, the other half were deflated and brown. The only good fruit, in my opinion, were maraschino cherries.

It wasn't until I was grown up and moved to the East Coast that I realized what truly delicious apples tasted like. We moved to California some years later and there I discovered the delight of sweet tree-ripened apricots and the wonder of fresh figs. I could hardly believe the bright-flavored fruit was what Fig Newton's were made of.

What makes fruit even better is that it is so very good for you. Usually, it seems the sweets I'm drawn to are really, really bad for me. Oh for vitamin-enriched Ho Hos, or a cancer-inhibiting custard-filled donut!

Fruits are the equivalent.

They are chock-full of antioxidants—nutrients such as vitamins, minerals, and enzymes that assist in chemical reactions that counteract the oxidization that occurs in our tissues. This oxidation is the equivalent of rusting in humans (otherwise known as aging), which means fruit is a pocket-sized fountain of youth! Fruit even plays cleanup to the free radicals zipping through our systems, looking to start a cancer party.

The caveat is that one must eat *whole* fruits. It's not going to work to suck down a carton of orange or apple juice. It is the combination of fruit's skin, flesh, and juice that gives it the punch; the ole "whole being greater than the sum of its parts" thing. An apple, for instance, has the greatest amount of antioxidants in its peel but has a great deal of soluble fiber via the pectin in its flesh. The good stuff in the peel and the flesh acts synergistically, resulting in a fruit that prevents metabolic disorders, high blood pressure, plaque buildup, and hardening of blood lipids. Apples inhibit cell proliferation (an anticancer effect) and lower the risk of heart attack and stroke.

Apple juice, however, has only 3 to 10 percent of the antioxidant activity and zero percent of the tantalizing crunch of whole apples.

There was no question that fruit would do a fine job providing good sweets; the question was, would I have enough? In fact, I was so worried about sating my sweet tooth, I made a grave gardening error with my little orchard. We had planted a baker's dozen of fruit trees in the backyard in two staggered rows along the back fence. The first row went as follows: a mission fig, a nectarine, a peach, a pear, an apple pear, a granny smith apple, and a fuyu persimmon. The second row had a green plum, a purple plum, a white fig, a mandarin orange, an apricot, and a cherry. We also had an orange and an olive tree at the north end of the yard, and a lemon and jujube tree at the south.

We planted most of them bare root, and for a time they remained the size of canes. After a couple of years some of them took off on a growth spurt, including a peach tree that became so prolific the set fruit looked like green pearls strung along the branches.

It is hard for me to thin fruit. In my mind, every thumbnail piece of fruit I popped off the branch was like throwing away a succulent grapefruit-sized freestone peach. It pained me to do it once, much less hundreds of times. Still, the books said I must clear them so that there was four inches between each piece of fruit. But there was the question: which pieces of fruit? The existing marble-sized fruit or the future full-grown fruit? The difference could mean many fewer bushels of peaches I'd get to harvest. I decided to go four inches between the marble-sized fruit.

As the fruit enlarged, however, the branches drooped further and further to the ground. I grew worried, but now thinning the fruit would have been a real waste—I'd be tossing out tennis ball-sized peaches, and I just couldn't bring myself to do that.

I stared at the tree and decided that I could prop up the branches. I'd get some notched two-by-fours and stick them under the groaning limbs. But even as I came up with that plan, the tree couldn't stand another minute of holding up the peaches. One of the two main branches cracked and, as I *watched*, peeled down the entire length of the tree. I screamed, "Nooo!" then the other main branch, weakened by the first branch decamping, cracked off as well. All that remained was a jagged trunk.

My peach tree had done itself in. I lost not only hundreds of peaches, but also several years of nurturing that went into the little peach tree, and the thousands and thousands and (sob) thousands of sweet, sticky, juicy peaches it would have given me in the years to come. While greed seems to pay off for corporations, it doesn't set so well with fruit.

If I wanted to keep my other trees healthy, not only was I going to have to do a better job of thinning the fruit, I would also need to learn how to prune the trees.

I found a small book at my local hardware store written in 1944 by R. Sanford Martin. In his back-of-the-book photo, Sanford looks like an old-fashioned bank employee who yearns to escape the confines of the institution and grow an orchard. His story, as well as the soulful look on his face, also hints at travails. He developed a process that revolutionized the treatment of gummosis in apricots—but the proceeds went to his employer. He worked with his parents on a citrus orchard until a tractor accident halted his work. Sanford was intrigued with humus production, but his ideas about the treatment of soils were ridiculed by the experts of the day, though eventually they were lauded.

This was enough to sell me on R. Sanford Martin, even if it turned out that the book was no good.

The book, however, was wonderful, filled with informative little sketches that Sanford drew indicating what branches to lop off when, and what a well-trained tree looked like. The best thing about the book is that it is specifically geared toward pruning for the home orchard rather than the commercial one, and he succinctly explains each cut that he recommends. "To one who understands how, where, and why a tree bears its fruit, pruning is an extremely simple job."

The pages on a peach tree begin, "There are few trees that benefit from heavy pruning as does the peach . . ." He goes on to say, "Do not hesitate to head back tall growth because peach wood is brittle and a tall tree is almost sure to shed otherwise good limbs when they are heavy with fruit." Oh Sanford, if I had only known.

Even without the peach tree, we had a calendar of fruit that stretched almost the entire year. The apricot was the first to provide in the spring. It was an exceptionally early-flowering tree. This was wonderful in the years there weren't late frosts, and a sad thing to lose the crop the years there were. As the apricots finished, cherries became ripe. When the cherries were done, the plums were ready, first purples then greens. Alongside plums came figs that provided throughout most of the summer, followed by pears, Asian pears, and apples in the late summer and early fall. In the late fall we had jujubes and persimmons. Then there was a stretch waiting for the oranges and mandarins to ripen, and another stretch between the last oranges in February and our early apricots, which I hover about, hardly able to bear waiting to taste the ripe fruit.

It's the birds that let me know when the fruit is ready. I don't know how they know but they, unlike me, never seem to start pecking before the produce is ripe. I generally waste an appalling amount of fruit biting hopefully into what isn't ready for consumption.

Though I appreciate the birds, I don't want to pay for their service with an entire tree of fruit, especially since the birds eat the fruit in a really annoying way. A quarter apricot here, a few pecks there, and then they let the rest drop to the ground and rot. If they'd eat the whole thing

I might be more magnanimous. Instead I searched for ways to foil the feathered thieves that didn't require me to sit under the tree with a stick or a shotgun.

I tried nets, and not only were they ugly and practically impossible for me to get on to the tree, but once on, the tangle of netting also effectively discouraged *me* from harvesting the fruit. The scarecrow I put up did nothing. I imagine the jays had seen scarier things when I walked around the yard in my bathrobe.

It was Goosteau who finally inspired a solution to the problem. I was standing in the goose yard, sipping a can of seltzer, when he suddenly attacked me. I know he is just a bird, but a goose attack is terrifying. Heck, a *wasp* is terrifying. There is something about furious pursuit that is so scary even when you know that when push comes to shove, you'll come out the winner with a squashed wasp underfoot.

I shouted, "Goosey, Goosey, GOOSEY!" hoping he'd come to his senses and stop battering me with his wings. Then I realized through the flurry of wings and wild honking that Goosteau was actually trying to save me from the can I held in my hand, which he apparently thought was attacking my lips. I threw the aluminum thing across the yard. Goosteau followed it and pummeled it with his beak until it was in tatters.

By that time Sam and Louis had come out of the house, and as we watched Goosteau kill the can we all feared he would either have a heart attack in his fury or slit his beak open on the sharp metal. I finally mustered my courage and gathered up the furious gander, tucking his huge wings under my arm as Sam dashed in and took the can away.

Like many birds, Goosteau is afraid of metallic objects, and he deals with his fear by trying to get rid of the offending item (or person.) Luckily other birds react differently or we'd all feel like Tippi Hedren in Hitchcock's *The Birds* every time we stepped out of our cars. Apparently many birds—especially the very intelligent corvids, and our perhaps not so brilliant waterfowl—have both neophilia and neophobia. That is, they are both attracted to *and* afraid of something new. This makes for a complex but intense reaction to novelty.

Using what we hoped was something that would engender the fruit-plundering blue jays' "phobic flight" response to shiny objects, we scrunched long pieces of aluminum foil along the cherry branches when the cherries approached harvest time.

Even though the aluminum foil was easy to both scrunch on (and to remove later), getting up to the higher branches was a little terrifying. As I wavered on the ladder fifteen feet up in a tree, contemplating a neck-snapping fall, I remembered that coconuts kill fifteen times as many people a year as sharks do. Fruit is dangerous business.

When I'd finished my scrunching, the aluminum-clad branches *did* look somewhat like metallic snakes loafing in the cherry tree, and the sunshine winking off the foil gave an illusion of movement. It must have looked that way to the birds, too. It kept the jays away for about two to three weeks—until they habituated to the foil.

Because they habituated so quickly, it was important to wait until the birds signaled the ready harvest before putting the foil on, and then to be sure to remove it immediately once the harvest was over so that it would work again the next year.

Most of the time, I didn't bother to scare critters away, especially if we had a large amount of fruit on the tree. Further, as the trees gained in height, the thought of climbing the trees was even more hair-raising. So while I'd rather the jays and squirrels didn't take all my fruit, I would certainly allow theft on the upper branches. I figure the birds have a right to some in return for eating bugs, entertaining the humans and the cats of the house, and providing their fruit-testing service.

There is a passage in Leviticus that says when you reap your harvest, do not reap the corners of the field. While I'm more pagan than anything, I do like that sentiment. Leave some for others; do not be greedy. I wonder if there is a passage in there somewhere that says to thin the fruit of your trees as well.

Candied Orange Peel Dipped in Chocolate

When I was a kid, my Grandma Streeter always had orange sticks for us to eat at Christmastime. The three-inch-long sticks of orange jelly enrobed in chocolate were about the diameter of a pencil, all perfectly alike as a factory-extruded food is expected to be, and absolutely delicious. We kids would pretend they were cigarettes and, making a mess of our fingers, sashay around like characters out of old movies. Alternately, we would suck all the chocolate off the jelly base until we were left with a transparent orange column that we would mash against the roofs of our mouths with our tongues until it disintegrated.

As an adult, however, I wasn't so crazy about the orange sticks. I had mostly grown past the stage of playing with my food, and the candies seemed too sweet, too untextured. Was it the cheap brand I bought, or was it my adult palate that made the difference? In any case, orange sticks were relegated to a delight of memory.

Then one Christmas a few years back, my neighbor brought over a holiday goody bag, and included alongside a number of cookies were some oddly shaped brown things. Frankly, they kind of looked like Christmas scat with a little orange tail sticking out. When I examined more closely, I discovered it was candied orange peel dipped in dark chocolate.

With some trepidation, I bit into it. And to my delight, I experienced the wonderful taste I remembered from my childhood, but one evolved to appeal to my grown-up mouth. The orange peel was intense and chewy, the dark chocolate sweet and deep. Heaven. Now I make my own, and it is amazingly easy.

I use the biggest navel oranges I can get off my tree. The rinds of Valencia oranges seem too thin, and I have even read recipes that instruct people to use a potato peeler to shave the orange peel from the oranges, but I think thick chewy rind makes the best candies. As for the pith, I'd like to say I remove it all before proceeding, but that would be grievously misrepresenting myself. I *do* scrape what seems like excess pith away for

aesthetic reasons, but I pretty much allow a lot of pith to remain not *only* because I am lazy but also because the pith contains the highest amount of antioxidants. I like my candy to be healthy. It also seems to me that the bitterness in the pith is taken care of when I blanch the peels. However, if you are a perfectionist, scrape away.

Ingredients:
- 6 navel Oranges
- 2 cups sugar
- 8 ounces dark chocolate

1. Using an orange scorer or paring knife, cut a cap at the top and bottom of each orange, leaving a girdle of rind around the middle of each orange.

2. Pare the girdle carefully away from the orange in squarish pieces, trying to keep the peel intact.

3. Use a spoon to scrape excess pith away, then place the squarish pieces of orange rind in a saucepan and cover with water.

4. Bring the peels and water to a boil, then drain and repeat two more times.

5. Cool the orange peels, then slice the squares into quarter-inch sticks.

6. Meanwhile, bring four cups of water to a boil, pour in the sugar, and allow to dissolve.

7. Place the orange sticks into the water and reduce heat to simmer lightly until the orange sticks are translucent. It will take anywhere from twenty minutes to more than an hour, depending on the peel. Don't stir the things. Doing so encourages crystal formation, and then you might have crunchy parts on your orange rinds.

8. When the orange sticks are translucent, use tongs to remove the sticks and place them on a sheet of parchment paper to dry. That can take hours or days, depending on humidity. If you want to speed things up, putting them in the dehydrator on low will do the trick.

Once dry, the orange sticks can be eaten as is, or chopped and used in baking for fruitcakes or panetone. But they are best dipped in melted dark chocolate. I like to dip the candied orange piece halfway up its length. Half bright orange and half brown looks nice to me and provides a good handle for dipping. When the chocolate is set, bag them up to give to friends and to freeze. You don't want easy access to them. They're just too tempting.

CIRCUS HENS

*"I did not become a vegetarian for my health.
I did it for the health of the chickens."*
—ISSAC BASHEVIS SINGER

According to the people who study this sort of thing, the first domesticated animals appeared in the Euphrates River Valley about ten thousand years ago. I imagine a Neolithic woman eyeing a goat (*Capra aegargus*), thinking, *I could catch that goat, easy. Too bad I've already eaten.* Then a new synapse fires and it occurs to her that she could catch the goat and save it for later. Maybe if she had a few of the creatures, they'd multiply and she wouldn't have to chase goats all over the Middle East every time she was feeling peckish. Hence, Neolithic farmers began keeping small herds of animals.

About eight thousand years ago, red junglefowl (*Gallus gallus*)—the flamboyantly feathered cousins of the pheasant—were domesticated as well, I'm guessing in much the same way. These fowl eventually evolved into the farmyard chickens of today (*Gallus domesticus*). Our earliest relationship with these animals was pretty straightforward. They were meat and we ate them. Then another bright guy figured out that animals could be used in other ways—for their milk, their wool,

their blood, their eggs—and he called his brainstorm the Secondary Products Revolution.

Jump ahead eight thousand years to a municipal park in Spearfish, South Dakota, one summer afternoon when I saw a girl, maybe twelve or thirteen years old, walk my way towing a wheeled cooler behind her. She had a large Wyandotte *Gallus domesticus* tucked under her arm. When she reached an open grassy area in the park, she put the chicken on the ground, sat on the cooler, and waited.

In short order, children spied the chicken calmly pecking at the grass. They were entranced at the basketball-sized animal who minded not at all a growing mob of shrieking children surrounding it, petting it, and making their own version of chicken noises. The girl desultorily answered questions. Yes it was a chicken. No, it didn't have a name. It *did* belong to her. Then, when the crowd's interest had dimmed a bit, she flung open the cooler, displaying an interior brimming with popsicles, and instructed the mob, "Ask your Mom for a quarter." She made a killing. Secondary Products Revolution indeed.

The chicken certainly seemed revolutionary to me. Other chickens I'd known had, perhaps, a bit too much *Gallus gallus* and not enough *Gallus domesticus* in them. They were ill-tempered, pecking each other bloody. They would never stand to be petted, though my brother learned to hypnotize a squawking chicken into flaccid idiocy by stroking its head at the base of the beak until it went cross-eyed and could be placed on its back, legs to the sky. Sometimes he could get half a dozen hens staged in ridiculous poses before they'd come back to their small chicken senses, roll over, and stagger back to business.

Back then I preferred ducks (not domesticated until 2500 BC), their rubber bills set in perpetual smile. Unfortunately so did raccoons. They would do anything for a taste: tunnel under the duck house or jimmy open a raccoon-proof latch. Once a raccoon pulled a duck through the wire grid of its pen, piece by piece. It was horrible. That was the last time I tried to raise ducks in Wyoming.

When I moved to California, I once again got ducks, certain they would be safer in town than at the ranch. Unfortunately, I found that urban California raccoons appreciated duck entrees as much as rural Wyoming ones did.

So we got the gander (domesticated 1500 BC) to protect the ducks, and with his mighty serrated beak and mightier honk, Goosteau has likely kept many a fowl murder from occurring. Additionally, he once alerted us to the presence of a drunken frat boy (not domesticated at all) who had scaled our fence at two in the morning on a mission to steal a farm animal for the glory of Alpha Omega.

We got our goose, Jeannette, to keep Goosteau company. As a perk she provides about thirty eggs a year, which, when colored, make awe-inspiring Easter gifts. Regardless of these merits, I would not recommend geese to anyone not living on a piece of land the size of Disneyworld. They are not just horrifically noisy, but noisy for a long, *long* time. The oldest known goose, "George" from the United Kingdom, lived forty-nine years, though the *New York Times* in 1907 reported a gander that lived to be seventy-one. I imagine George might have lived longer, but someone likely throttled him so they could sleep in on a Sunday morning.

Further complicating matters was finding that ducks only lived about six years, so the pairing of duck and goose was a poorly proportioned relationship, kind of like pouring a gallon of milk on a cup of fruit loops.

Worst of all, however, is the fact that the geese are ornery. When he was eight, Sam insinuated himself into Goosteau's good graces by standing in the house and feeding the gander one peanut after another through the window. Louis, however, did not get along with Goosteau at all. Maybe it was Louis's beard that put Goosteau off, or maybe it was Goosteau's nature to make a lot of loud noise and refuse to back down—it certainly was Louis's. Any time Louis went into the backyard, Goosteau's head would drop and he would attack. I sometimes found my husband holding Goosteau's beak shut in self-defense while the gander squonked and flapped in fury, both of them unwilling to give.

I loved Goosteau. Louis didn't.

Such complex interactions between man and animal have played out over and over since that day in the Euphrates River Valley. In fact, in the early nineteenth century there were more divorces among the Pawnee over horses than any other reason. Pawnee men loved horses. Ownership of them was a mark of prestige as well as an advantage to crossing more ground in a hurry. Pawnee women, however, hated them because horses ate their gardens.

Louis and I managed to navigate the problem of Goosteau just as I imagine the Pawnees did the problem of horses—through containment. We gave the geese their part of the yard and the humans took the other.

When I decided to rely on the Quarter-Acre Farm to eat, yet another problem made itself apparent. Both the remaining duck and the goose were relatively poor egg layers; geese are bred to be meat animals. People apparently prefer eggs in single-serving sizes, not the economy size that geese produce. Besides, Jeannette only laid her monumental eggs one to two months of the year and our remaining duck, Sunny, was in her declining years. Living off the Quarter-Acre Farm necessitated that I have eggs to eat year round. Eggs, along with legumes, would be one of my prime sources of protein. Eggs also provide a myriad of other nutrients including folate, iron, zinc, and choline.

Odd that I didn't *remember* ever hearing of choline before, but apparently eggs are second only to beef liver in providing it. Research shows that only one out of ten Americans gets enough choline, which aids not only in the transport of nutrients through the body but also in brain and memory development. Ah.

Eggs were obviously important. To that end, friends who had a ranchette on which they raised pigs, wine grapes, horses, and chickens, offered to give me two of their laying hens. Their chickens had a wonderful setup, with a cozy henhouse and the run of several acres. Those chickens did not know how good they had it.

Once upon a time, people raised chickens in small flocks. Up until

World War II, most eggs came from flocks of fewer than four hundred hens. Today, flocks of one hundred thousand are more typical, with flocks of more than a million hardly unusual. Incubation farms hatch chicks, which are then sent on to egg farms and meat farms where hens face crowded conditions and are often debeaked to prevent cannibalism. In California, a groundbreaking law passed requiring that chickens be housed with *enough room to turn around*. A sad victory.

Our friends' hens had a few acres to turn around in and therefore were rather difficult to catch. In the end, we managed to snare a barred Plymouth Rock hen (who had an unnervingly bare posterior, which eventually sprouted a profusion of downy feathers) and a Rhode Island Red. Our friends promptly upended both chickens and dusted them with delousing powder. We popped the hens into a laundry basket, bungeed another basket on top, stuck the whole shebang in the back seat, and drove back to town.

Sam shared the back seat with the chickens. We reminded him how lucky he was. While one of his best friends flew to Nicaragua that summer, another to New York City to watch a play on Broadway, Sam got to visit North Dakota *and* drive across rural California with louse-dusted, red-butted poultry beside him.

Back at the Quarter-Acre Farm, we introduced the chickens to the wheeled chicken house Sam and I had built out of plywood and an old garden cart. The house had two rooms (one for nesting, one for perching) two sections of roof that opened, and a front wall that lifted entirely for cleaning. Sam primed the chicken house and applied a coat of brilliant blue. The door of the house served as a ramp and opened into the chicken tunnel, which was a long propylene net stretched over three copper pipe supports. We could roll the chicken house to different locations around the garden as needed, stretch the chicken tunnel in front of it, and let the chickens out. The chickens would scratch to their heart's content while tilling and fertilizing the plot at the same time.

It worked like a charm. Sam named the hens Klio and Kalliopi after the muses of history and music. Just as one hopes muses will be, they were productive, each laying about five eggs a week. That meant the chickens were working at the top of their game since it takes about thirty-four hours for a hen to produce an egg.

The best eggs have a thick albumen (egg white)—the source of egg riboflavin and protein—that stands high and is differentiated from the thin albumen located nearer the shell that spreads around the thick white. In grade AA eggs, the "chalazae," which are the cord-like strands of egg white that anchor the yolk in the center of the egg, are prominent (the more prominent the chalazae, the fresher the eggs). The yolk is firm, round, and high. This described our eggs perfectly, and further, our yolks were so orange they tinted the dinner rolls we made a pale yellow. Of course, the reason the eggs that came out of our hens were so good was because of what went *into* the hens.

Chickens will eat practically anything, including leftover oatmeal, greens, meat scraps, polenta, pizza—the combination of which provides them a pretty decent diet. Further, it allows them to fit perfectly into our recycling program. What we didn't eat went to the hens, and what the hens didn't eat went on to the compost; the compost went into the garden, and what the garden grew went into the frittata, and what we didn't eat of the frittata went back into the hens.

Along with scraps, we also fed our chickens a daily treat of birdseed, which they threw all over the pen in their haste to get the one particular kind of seed that was their favorite. They then spent the rest of the day plucking the second-rate seeds strewn on the ground. Cracked corn supplemented the grass, worms, and weeds they scratched up from where their house was parked that week.

Even though it seemed our chickens were egg-laying machines, I knew that hens went into a slump for a time in the winter. I decided to bank my eggs against just that possibility. (Properly refrigerated, eggs last a long time. Some say up to five months. If you wonder about the age of the egg, put it in a glass of water. Newer eggs sink and older ones float. There is an air cell in the large end of each egg that's caused by the contraction of the egg's contents as it cools after the hen lays it. It continues to increase with the egg's age. Thus, more air means more floating means older egg.)

Just to be safe, I also froze some eggs. I cracked open the shells then stirred the white and yolk together and put them into ice cube trays to freeze. If you want to separate the white and yolk, the white will freeze fine on its own. The yolk, however, will become lumpy with freezing. To counteract that, stir either salt or sugar in with the yolks (making sure to mark them for either sweet or savory dishes) before sticking them in the freezer. They should last up to a year.

With all these eggs, I felt free to make omelets, eggs in a nest, fritters, frittatas, and pancakes. I also hard-boiled them, scrambled them, put them in baked goods, and best of all, made my famous (or it *should* be famous) French toast. Even if my hens suddenly stopped laying, I would be able to continue doing so for a couple of weeks.

I was pleased with my preparations, and with the eggs themselves, but what really pleased me were the chickens. As I said, I had never really liked chickens, but now I was smitten. Why? Maybe it was because they were feeding me; I could love a black widow spider if it skittered over with breakfast on its carapace. Yet I think it more likely that I had never really gotten to know the chickens from my childhood.

Louis, Sam, and I spend a lot of time in the garden, and therefore a lot of time with the hens, watching them, talking to them, feeding them bits of food. Hens have about thirty different utterances including separate calls for danger approaching from over land, water, and air. Listening carefully, we sussed out the "something good to eat" cluck, the "back off" cluck, the contented cluck, the "watch the cat" cluck, the "Hey, I've laid an egg!" cluck, and my favorite, the pleased greeting trill.

A large vocabulary wasn't our chickens' only attraction, it turned out.

We referred to Klio and Kalliopi as the circus hens because they would leap a foot off the ground to grab a grape from your fingers. I took everyone who came to the house into the back for a demonstration, as proud of the chickens had they written their names in the dust with their yellow beaks. Even the cats were intrigued. The old cat, Pippin—who, to keep her from killing birds, had been weighted with so many bells during her prime that she looked like a bit player from Spartacus—gazed at the hens as if they were cat TV.

I soon found I was not alone in my appreciation for hens. Surfing the Internet I found hundreds of sites dedicated to chickens. There are sites that will walk you through every aspect of chicken ownership, including chicken nutrition, chicken housing, and navigating city codes if your burg frowns on fowl. And if I thought I was smitten with my chickens, I soon realized I was comparatively inattentive. There are websites where you can buy toys for your chickens, little bags of organic treats, chicken *clothing*. I saw videos of chicken owners pushing their hens about in prams. And to see someone kiss their chicken, and someone else give CPR and mouth-to-beak resuscitation to a hen, and to watch the excellent *The Natural History of the Chicken*, written and directed by Mark Lewis—you'll never look at a hen in the same way again.

In terms of talent, it turned out that my chickens were comparative duds. Apparently other chickens can play the piano, for Pete's sake. But I still adored Klio and Kalliopi. In turn, the chickens seemed to like us as much as we liked them, which easily made up for their lack of musical ability. When we went into the backyard, Klio and Kalliopi would press against the net like groupies greeting the Grateful Dead. Their happiness was endearing. I looked forward to moving their chicken house to a new location every few weeks because when I let them out, they would tumble down the ramp and look around them in apparent awe that the world had changed overnight.

No matter their delight in the world, when the sun stopped shining as brightly, their egg production did indeed drop markedly. By December, it had stopped altogether. I didn't panic, for I had my hoarded eggs, and I had a plan.

I installed a solar light, one of those designed to illuminate a garden path. I cut a hole in the chicken house roof, fit the lamp in, caulked it, introduced the chickens, and waited for the eggs to pile up. Nothing happened. As one eggless day followed another, and the number of my hoarded eggs dwindled, I stopped having boiled eggs for lunch, and then stopped baking. I only allowed myself to dip my bread into half an egg for my French toast, and even that was drawing to a close.

In the meantime my friends told me that the chickens in the country flock were laying as if they were the muses of omelets. Feeling embarrassed for my circus hens, I admitted that my chickens had given up eggs for the winter. I described the installation of the light. My friend told me it was natural for the hens to have a rest from egg laying, and I could indeed nudge them back into production. However, my little solar bulb was too dim. So I pried the solar light from the chicken house roof and replaced it with a 100-watt bulb.

The first time I turned on the light, the chickens were confused.

At dusk they went in to roost. But inside, their house was bright as day, so they came out. They stood perplexed in the deepening night, turned around and went back in, then came back out again. So it went until I finally unplugged the light, let them settle on their roosts, shut the door, and then plugged the light back on. Within 48 hours, the girls were laying again, and I was enjoying my favorite full-egg French toast breakfast every morning. French toast that I like to think Louis and Sam might leap a foot off the ground for and pluck the plate right from my fingers.

Walnut French Toast

For each piece of French toast you will need one slice of bread, the type of which is up to you. I like a dense multigrain variety, or for a fancier version, a slice of brioche. You will also need as much sliced fruit as you like to eat at one sitting, and a handful of chopped walnuts.

We use gleaned walnuts. A friend has about fifty huge trees on one section of her farm. The trees are so huge they are not commercially viable to pick, nor are the walnuts of a type that the commercial buyers are in the market for. Too bad for them, but great for us. At the end of the summer, armed with empty paint buckets and burlap sacks, we go out with several other families and pick enough of the walnuts to tide us over the entire year. The hard part is shelling them. We tried a dozen different nut crackers before we found the best method. Our neighbor Jay gifted us with an eight-inch-high, four-inch-wide section of log with a divot in the middle. I put the end of the walnut in the divot and smack the walnut with a hammer, just enough to break the shell but not enough that the nut loses shape. Louis and I sit on the porch like two old people, me putting a walnut on the divot, him wacking and tossing the cracked nut into a bowl. Fifteen minutes and you've got a week of French toast, cookies, and snacks—and the birds eat the bits that get left behind.

The key to this French toast is that during cooking you allow the eggs to set. This "glues" the walnuts into place so that when the toast is flipped, the walnuts don't abandon the bread. Therefore you want a nice low heat and a cover for your skillet.

Ingredients (for each slice of toast):
- 1 slice of bread
- 1 egg
- 1 heaping tsp brown sugar
- ⅛ tsp vanilla
- dash of salt
- ⅛ cup chopped walnuts
- fruit (as much as you'd like)

1. Beat the egg(s), vanilla, brown sugar, and salt until frothy. If the eggs seem too thick to soak into the bread, add a bit of milk.

2. Dip both sides of the bread in the egg mixture and place into an oiled skillet on a low-medium heat.

3. Throw the chopped walnuts into the remaining egg mixture, stir, then quickly pour this mixture evenly onto the upward-facing side(s) of the bread in the skillet. Use your spatula to *press* the chopped walnuts into the soggy bread.

4. Cover the skillet but frequently check the underside of the toast for color. When it is golden brown, *gently* flip the toast to brown the walnut-encrusted side.

5. When that is nicely brown as well, slide the bread onto plates, turn the burner up to medium high, throw the fruit into the skillet with some water and, depending on the sweetness of your fruit and your own taste, add in some optional brown sugar and let it simmer briskly until the fruit has become soft, and the water, juice, and sugar have combined into syrup. Pour fruit and syrup over the toast.

A dollop of Greek yogurt or fresh ricotta on the top of the steaming fruit pushes this meal into nirvana. If you eat this dish at half past 10 in the morning, it can almost get you through until dinner.

FREE STUFF

*"No unemployment insurance can be compared
to an alliance between man and a plot of land."*
—HENRY FORD

One of the criticisms I hear most about gardening is the cost. A magazine or newspaper will run an article refuting gardening's cost effectiveness, tallying the cost of seeds, dirt, raised beds, and the like, concluding that a home-grown tomato must cost somewhere in the range of a new Subaru.

Well sure it can, but not if you're cheap like me. I am the kind of person who is drawn to magazines that announce "Remodel for pennies!" Or, "Can't afford a new kitchen? You can with this plan!" Or, "Low Budget, no problem!" The trouble is that most of the time "pennies" means tens of thousands of dollars, and my idea of a low budget isn't *Elle Décor's*. So it goes with gardening too.

My idea of gardening is that I will eat well, enjoy myself, and save money. In order to save money, I need to garden on a budget. A Spring Warren budget. Which is minimal. In order to stay in that budget I use a lot of free and cheap stuff to garden with.

Cheap doesn't have to mean ugly. I (and my neighbors and family)

don't want the garden filled with failed retreads that I'm using as raised beds. Planting in an old toilet might be cute in some people's yards, but I'd rather not have one in mine. I am cheap, but I'm also picky. This would seem to create a quandary, except that there are so many ways to get by using inexpensive or even free items.

The number one way to get garden stuff is to have garden friends; be in a gardening loop. I have been luckier than anyone has a right to be and have often benefited from a friend's interest in improving her garden or trying something new. When old bricks are replaced by new pavers, I am often happily offered the bricks. I got my first wooden raised beds because a friend began using a new bed system. Gravel, top soil, plants, seeds, growing plastic, pots, trellises, and river rock have all made their way to me via friends.

If you check Craigslist, you will find all sorts of cheap and free stuff. "Cart away the fill dirt and it's yours." "Peeler poles for a dollar each." "If you take chickens today, you can have them no charge (landlord is complaining)."

In many cities there is a Freecycle group. The Freecycle Network has almost five thousand groups, so chances are good there are Freecyclers near you. It is a nonprofit entity that facilitates its members getting and giving things away for free, promoting reuse of items and keeping useable goods from ending up in the landfill. People post not only what they'd like to get rid of, but also things they need. I recently scrolled down a list of things to give away and this is what I found: mums, garden hoses, plant buckets and pots, mustard greens, gravel, garden stones, wooden boxes on wheels, shade canopy, irrigation fittings, and for those of you who *do* like whimsy—several toilets. I myself have been gifted a dwarf peach tree, organic potting soil, gloves, tools, and a big bag of asparagus crowns. Membership is of course free.

This sort of turnaround is one of the perks of farming in town. In the country, old stuff gets put in the barn or in the might-need-that-again-someday junk pile full of rusting baling wire, spools, a rusting truck body, cinderblocks, churn bodies, and who knows what else. There isn't that kind of space in town, and it costs money to get rid of excess. Giving it away or selling it for a song is a win-win situation for everyone.

For instance, I have spread truckloads and truckloads and truckloads of free mulch in my yard. Store-bought mulch is almost always a chipped or shredded redwood. It is a warm sienna color for a time and then fades into a sun-washed grey brown. My mulch is free and it is never a warm sienna color, nor of a homogenous texture. Instead, it is a mixture of browns and greens and has a variety of textures because it comes from the tree-trimming companies that work in my town. The mulch is the chipped branches that are pruned from all varieties of trees. The tree-trimming companies are pleased to dump an entire truckload of mulch in my driveway; it means they bypass a trip to the dump, along with the dump fees. While this mulch isn't a consumer-familiar color or texture, leaves are mulched up along with the branches and bark, which makes for a much healthier mineral-rich application. Because it's free, I can be very generous with the depth of mulch I put into my yard, which means that after the many truckloads of mulch I have spread across the Quarter Acre Farm, I now have a very generous layer of humus on the ground.

Still, I know that redwood mulch looks nice, perhaps nicer than my free stuff (though I could make an argument against that). Further, I have to admit that I am a fan of cocoa hulls, which are not only a beautiful dark brown, but smell like chocolate heaven as well. If one wants the color or the smell of purchased mulch but the cost of the free stuff, I recommend putting down eight to twelve inches of the free stuff and then broadcasting a film of the redwood bark/cocoa hulls over the top.

Speaking of trees, pay attention to events. Arbor Day is a great day to pick up free trees. In my town on picnic day in the spring you can get free vegetable starts. Free pumpkins are given away at the fall farmers' market festival and often those Halloween-y and fall-themed yard decorations end up in the garbage unless you mention you would love to take those bales of straw off their hands and use them to winterize your beds, bed your animals, or add to your compost.

Compost is expensive but homemade compost is free. Many communities give away free composters through their recycling programs, but if not, they're easy to build. My neighbors built theirs from discarded wooden shipping pallets. (Free how-to-build-your-own instructions can be found in many places on the web.) If you don't have access to pallets, there's no law that says a compost pile can't just decompose au naturel.

Manure is free if you have livestock. If not, perhaps you know some-one who does. Lots and lots of people have rabbits for pets. Ask them to dump their pans of wood shavings and bunny berries into a bucket for you. If you want a lot of rabbit manure, look up rabbitries on the Internet or ask your local pet store (or butcher) where they get their rabbits from. Likely as not, a rabbit-raising entity will happily give away the manure for free, or at least at a very minimal charge if they're seeing manure as a crop in itself.

Some say that feeding animals costs money, so therefore manure isn't free. True, but you can get free feed for your critters—feed your live-stock discards from the grocery store. Louis calls the co-op several times a week and asks for a box of green trimmings. He is in competition with several other people (including "J," the other goose lady) who do the same thing. The trick is to call first thing in the morning. What we get in the boxes is varied. It is a good day when there are mild greens in the box. The geese, the duck, the chickens, and the rabbits all love lettuces. Rab-bits and chickens love the fruit, but none of the animals likes mustard greens or kales, nor will they eat garlic or onions in any form. Potatoes are not popular, but if they sprout I can use them for seed. What we can't feed the animals we put into the compost pile to feed the bacteria and worms that make the dirt.

That's not the only garden-related stuff you can get from your gro-cery store. I get my best growing beans (cranberry and pintos) from my organic grocery. I bought them in a pinch and have bought them by choice since. I also buy sprouted chickpeas from the grocery store. You're supposed to use them in salads but since chickpeas can be a bother to sprout and the sprouted chickpeas are marked half-price after a day or two, they're often cheaper than a packet of seeds.

When my potatoes sprout in the refrigerator, I see it as an audition for growth. If they sprout in the fridge, I figure they'll do pretty good outside, and so far, that's proven out. These are organic potatoes. Conventional potatoes are often sprayed with a sprout inhibitor, maleic hydrazide, which inhibits cell division in plants. I got a potato in the discarded greens for the geese and tossed it aside, and the thing still looked and felt like a rock after a month out in the sun. And we are supposed to eat those?

Sweet potatoes are different. In fact, they aren't exactly potatoes; they are more closely related to morning glories, so they are propagated a bit differently. If you want to grow sweet potatoes, give yourself at least a month's head start; stick a raw sweet potato halfway into a jar of water. It will root and grow shoots (called slips). Twist the four- to six-inch slips from the potato, stick them in a jar of water, and when the slips get roots they're ready to plant in the ground and grow bushels of lovely sweet potatoes.

Nurseries often pile their six packs of wilted vegetable and flower seedlings in a corner to throw away. If you ask, sometimes they'll give the perceived goners to you. A little TLC and the sad little plants will either come around or they'll die entirely. If you're willing to gamble, it can work out well. Jesse brought home a tarp full of discarded flowers. I stuck them everywhere, willy-nilly, telling the bedraggled plants, "This is it, your last chance, pull yourself up by your chlorophyll-green bootstraps." Lots of the blooms rallied and provided the farm with beauty and beneficial insects. Some noticed they didn't have bootstraps and died, but some of the dead came back the next spring as if they'd just been resting for nine months.

I also get free plants from my garden, all the time—from volunteers and rooting shoots. My rosemary plants are parents to hundreds of little rosemary plants. If you trim plants in the spring when the new branches are still pliant, you can dip their cut ends in rooting hormone and stick them in the dirt. You can also bend a branch down and cover it with dirt. In no time they will be newly rooted bushes.

You also can get water for free. My parents have several vinyl-sided pools that fill up with rainwater by early summer and then are depleted little by little as rains ebb and flow and ebb and ebb. . . . My friends Alan and Emily just put in rain barrels that collect the rain that comes out of their roof gutters. Alan and Emily are heroes of mine because not only do they catch rain, but when they run their shower and wait for the water to heat, they also use buckets to catch the initial cold water and use it in the yard.

I have begun to use a bucket in the kitchen to wash produce, loathe to pour good water down the hatch (and gunk up the drains with dirt and aphids). Even more, though, I dream of utilizing a greywater recycling system—even if just to capture the sink water that runs down the drain with nothing but toothpaste in it, or the water from our washing machine, since we use phosphate-free soap.

Another thing that's available for free, but only after you're a *together* farmer (something I still haven't managed to become), is seed from your own vegetables. I keep meaning to put together a system, not only to collect seed (and *remember* to collect them), but also to date, store, and then remember (once again) that I've got the seeds to plant. Maybe this year.

Then there's free produce, a movement started by my neighbor Judith. She simply set out a cardboard box and wrote "FREE" on one of the flaps with a Sharpie. Inside the box she'd put her extra lemons. I've gotten so used to going down the street to get lemons when I'm out, that I'm somewhat surprised when I see them for sale at the grocery store.

After the lemon box came the Great Pineapple Guava Giveaway by Millicent, then the Peach Purge by Bridgette. Louis went back and picked Hayashi persimmons off the student rental behind us, and I have given bowls of tomatoes away, spears and spears of rosemary for grilling, peppers, and fruit.

One of the great pleasures of a garden is sharing the produce. Some people would rather get their produce frozen or plastic wrapped, especially if they object to the odd slug in the lettuce or a chew hole in the basil. That's okay, but to other people, a garden gift is heaven. And because they appreciate the produce you give them (or the homemade marmalade), they will give you some of what they grow too, or perhaps the oranges with which to make marmalade, or maybe some dirt in order to grow an orange tree, or even the manure to feed it.

Rough French Tart

I was on the phone to my father one afternoon while I was peeling apples. I told him I was making a tart and then asked him if he had ever made a rough French tart. There was a pause on the other end of the line and then he said, "No, but I always hoped I'd have the opportunity."

Though this tart is rough as they come, I make it for the guys at the spur of the moment, often when calamities strike and we're in the need of tenderness. A few apples anointed with sugared cinnamon are baked until fragrant and soft on a bed of flaky, buttery crust. It is true comfort food—ready to ease anxieties over deadlines, ennui, or general political outrage.

I also make this tart when *good* things happen, like when free apples come around. My friend Lisa has called upon me several times to save her from the deluge of excess Fuji apples she has hanging on her tree, and I am always happy to oblige—just to help a friend out.

This tart takes virtually no time, just peel a few apples, make a crust, and voila! French tart. (Especially if you've got a food processor to help with the crust.)

Ingredients:

- 3 to 4 apples
- ⅛ cup chopped walnuts
- ½ cup butter
- 1½ cups flour
- ⅛ cup sugar
- 3 to 4 TB sugar for sprinkling (coarse sanding sugar is extra pretty)
- 1 tsp salt

The key to a good crust is to leave chunks of butter in the dough—that is, *not* to work the dough until the butter and flour are well mixed together—so a few pulses with the processor are all that's needed. The butter in the pastry melts while baking and the resulting spaces in the pastry are what make the pastry crisp and crumbly. If there are no chunks of

butter to leave vacancies in the pastry and instead you've got homogenized dough, you'll end up with tough crust.

1. Put the flour, sugar, and salt in the processor, whir it a couple of times to make sure it is all mixed, then dump in the cold butter (which I typically cut into roughly half-inch dice).

2. Pulse the processor a couple of times, then add some water, pulse again, add a bit more and pulse again. I do this until the dough is just holding together, then pull it out and refrigerate it.

3. When the dough is cold, roll it out into a (rough) circle. Pre-heat the oven to 375 degrees. Slice the apples and arrange them in the circle.

4. When I'm making the tart, I might then sprinkle some chopped walnuts over the apples next since apple season happens to correspond with the new crop of walnuts that we glean from our friend Joannie's orchard. (Fruits and vegetables that come ripe at the same time often are the things that taste best together.)

5. Sprinkle the apples (and walnuts, if you add them) with sugar and cinnamon.

6. Fold the lip of the pastry over the apples along the edge, then sprinkle a little more sugar on the lipped edge of the crust.

7. Put the tart in a 375-degree oven and bake until the pastry is lightly browned.

It won't fix everything, but it seems to for the time it takes to eat it.

MUD

With all of the digging and planting, uprooting, flicking, and canning, I was ready for a break. My friend Sally found a spa up the road in Calistoga that wasn't too pricey. We made a reservation for the mud bath/massage package.

I had never had a mud bath or a massage. At least not a massage given to me by a stranger. Growing up in Wyoming, "going to a massage parlor" meant something entirely different than getting a back-rub. Now that I lived in California, where chair massages are not only offered at the grocery store, but having a massage therapist arrive at the office as a perk for your employees comes as easily as if you were ordering up a bouncehouse for a children's party, it was time to give the spa life a try.

However, as soon as Sally made the reservations, I started to worry. Not about the massage. It was the idea of the mud bath that was torturing me. What kind of mud was it in the bath, and more importantly, was it *fresh* mud? I asked Louis about it incessantly. Although he had about as much knowledge of spa mud as our cats did, I still badgered him into assuring me that of course it would be fresh.

"Because I wouldn't want to get in someone's used mud!" I shuddered. "To think of what could be in there. Skin flakes if you want to hold your imagination in check, but let it go and you could see how there could be . . ."

"It will be fresh mud!" he said again and again.

There are many spas in Calistoga, and when Sally and I arrived in town we wandered for some time searching for the one we'd made our reservation at. Eventually, we found the sign in front of a grand Victorian mansion, lawn trimmed to perfection, relaxed people in linen and loafers loafing on the porch. However, when we tried to check in, we were told we were in the wrong place—*our* spa was around the corner.

Around the corner was a strip mall, and in that strip mall, sure enough—our spa. Making the best of it, we ducked inside. After checking in, we were directed to our mud baths.

In my most pleasant reveries, I had envisioned reclining in a claw-footed tub, enrobed in warm silky mud that was much like melted milk chocolate. (Okay, in my most pleasant reveries it actually *was* chocolate.) It was anything but. Not only did the mud look like a rather chunky slurry of horse manure, but it also smelled like sulfur. Worst of all, it came in two gigantic vats that obviously could only be changed with a crane and a cadre of weightlifters. This was most certainly not new mud.

Sally and I looked at each other and commenced nervous giggling. Then, under the polite pressure of the spa attendant, we each disrobed and got into our vat. The slurry was so thick we had to energetically wriggle our naked selves into the muck. As soon as the attendant left I began whining, "How many people have been in this mud before us, do you think? The temperature of this mud must be ideal for bacteria . . . and intestinal parasites, come to think of it. Who would ever believe, if it were to happen, that we got an STD in a tub full of dirt?"

Sally leapt from the vat and into the shower before the attendant showed up with our fizzy water.

I've thought a lot about that mud, about how mud baths are supposed to not only relax a person but also clean out the pores, improve the complexion, relieve joint and muscle pain, and remove toxins. Is there something to it? People all over the world seem to believe so.

At the 3 Healing Lagoons in Chilca, outside of Lima, Peru, people slather themselves with greenish-colored mud that is said to heal not only skin ailments, acne, rheumatism, and arthritis, but also ailments of the eyes, nerves, and joints; it's also said to lower blood pressure, increase fertility, cure bone ailments, provide relief from diabetes, and increase the odds that a woman will bear twins. The muds of Techirghiol, Romania, promise more reasonable results: general skin healing and a state of well-being and relaxation. Believers of geophagy from many nations say that eating pure, finely milled bentonite clays will pull impurities from your entire system and will bind and eliminate toxins. There are recipes available, such as clay brownies, to make eating the stuff more toothsome. (I myself would eat carpet fluff if it were imbedded in a brownie.)

Some muds are specialized clay mixtures, others peat moss and volcanic ash. Sapropelic muds are supposed to be especially therapeutic and are composed of decaying matter dredged from the bottom of a body of water. Just the name, composed from the Greek words "sapros" and "pelos," meaning "putrefaction" and "earth," are enough to put me off.

I take for granted that dirt is going to wreak havoc on my skin rather than heal it. In fact, I thought a friend was giving me a gardener's viewpoint when she quoted, "My flesh is clothed in the filth of dust, my skin is withered and drawn together." She gave me one of those kinds of looks then told me it was Job's lament from the bible, and no, he hadn't been weeding.

Most days, millions of other tillers of the soil and I have at least our hands and feet in the mud of farms and gardens, and I am sure we actually ingest a bit of it as we go about our business. But I have trouble with seeing it as a miracle cure. Though spa mud is expected to do wonderful things for a person, no one points out the loveliness of, say, a farmer's cuticles nor the dewy smoothness of their skin. Further, there are truckloads of gardener's products available for purchase that are meant to *rescue* one from the effects of mud on the skin—from cuticle cream and soaps to barrier and healing lotions. As often as the free market sells you on the miracles of mud, it will sell you a cure for it as well.

Some cures are more necessary than others. Say you find mud immersion to be so fine you want to not only relax in the stuff, but to pitch battle in it as well. You might then consider the sport of mud wrestling. If so, keep this in mind—two hundred participants in a mud festival in South Korea were taken to the hospital because their skin was inflamed. Seven students from the University of Washington who had been wrestling in mud made from soil purchased from a gardening store developed hundreds of red, pus-filled dots afterward. All suffered from a syndrome called *dermatitis palaestrae limosae,* or dermatitis of muddy wrestling, in which bacteria penetrated their skin through hair follicles. Mud can be dangerous stuff.

On the other hand, the farmers I know do tend to be pretty upbeat for folks constantly facing down soilborne skin diseases. Considering the amount of work they do, the worries over the weather and the market, and the wretched state of their cuticles, this attitude can be remarkable. But mud, once again, may be part of that sunny persona.

Neuroscience, Medical News Today and *Discover Magazine,* to name a few, have all reported on intriguing studies concerning the effects of a soil bacterium called *Mycobacterium vaccae.* Apparently the bacteria activate serotonin-releasing neurons in the brain (as does Prozac) to elevate mood. Further, inoculation with the soil bacterium can also activate immune cells, improve asthma, and ease allergies.

The Marquis de Sade, a figure I would not as a matter of course turn to for life instruction, did say, "Miserable creatures, thrown for a moment on the surface of this little pile of mud . . . is it for you to pronounce on what is good and what is evil?" I will submit, in reference to mud among much else, that such pronouncements are *not* for me. While my fingers suffer hangnails and my skin calluses, I will yet not denigrate mud.

In fact, all things considered—the aforementioned mood-elevating properties added to the ongoing exercise a farmer is getting, the good food growing, some sunshine, a little meditative weeding—I would say one might consider farming one's very own spa treatment.

One ideally followed by a good hot bath and a great massage.

Mud Truffles

The idea of mud truffles came to me as I read about seed bombs. What are seed bombs? They are a weapon of mass beauty used by Guerilla Gardeners—which is a movement started by the late Liz Christy to bring debilitated, abandoned (and off limits) land back to verdancy. The Guerilla Gardeners encase wildflower seeds into balls of mud and compost, then lob the balls (or seed bombs) into abandoned lots. With time and rain, the seeds sprout and transform the barren lots into wild-flower-covered oases.

If you check online, you'll find hundreds of recipes for seed bombs that include material such as powdered clay, compost, leaf mold, and seeds, which is all mixed with water then formed into balls. Easy as (mud) pie. Why not just throw the seeds? Covering the seeds allows them to become heavy enough to throw and gives the seeds some good dirt to get a start on growing.

Interestingly, the idea of seed bombs is not only attractive to guerilla-type gardeners. Seed companies also make them, but they call *their* bombs pelletized seeds. The seeds are covered with clay, sometimes fertilizer, sometimes an inoculant. Covering seeds in this way allows farmers to space their seed more effectively, cutting down on crowded, undersized, strangely shaped vegetables as well as eradicating the time it would take for thinning. Pelletized seeds, just like seed "bombs," offer better targeting and better germination.

However, big seed companies are not sitting around in tie-dyed T-shirts rolling seeds into mud balls. Most big companies borrowed their seed pelletizing process from candy companies. The seed is covered the same way a Jordan almond is covered in its candy shell—tumbled in a drum in which a sticky substance is blown, followed by a blast of powdered clay (or clay and inoculants/fertilizer, etc.) then more stickiness and more powder until a shell of sufficient thickness is agglomerated.

This mélange of seeds and mud and candy gave me the idea for what I like to call mud truffles. All that's needed to make them are seeds, a good potting soil mix, and clay. Because they are going in the garden, (which you have prepared with fluffy rich soil) there is no need to add compost (humus) or fertilizer. I use mostly good garden soil so the mud truffles don't turn into hard clay prisons for the seeds—they will be porous enough to uptake water, fall apart, and allow the seeds to flourish.

Ingredients:

- 1 cup garden soil
- ⅛ cup powdered clay
- seeds (of your choice)
- water

1. Mix the garden soil with the powdered clay and mix with a little water until you have some good, damp (not sodden) mud.

2. Roll into a ball (use a melon scooper for perfect sizing).

3. Press a seed (carrot, lettuce, bean—practically any of them will work great) into the formed ball, and let it dry.

That's it. Of course, it would be much more truffle-like if you also dipped your soil sphere into some white sand or mild granulated organic fertilizer to look prettier. Some mini paper candy cups and a ribboned box to house an assortment of mud truffles, along with instructions to merely lay the truffles on the prepared bed in the correct spacing when the spring rains come, would make a really easy and incredibly charming gift for your garden-averse friends. It may inspire them to start gardening and could also encourage more home-growing food across the planet!

THE MYSTERIOUS UNDERGROUND

*"What I say is that, if a fellow really likes potatoes,
he must be a pretty decent sort of fellow."*
—A.A. MILNE

When I was a kid, my folks let us stay up as late as we wanted on Friday nights to watch "monster movies." My sister and I would huddle on the sofa in the basement and have the heck scared out of us by Dracula, the Blob, or Frankenstein. It was at the end of one of those nights, sometime past midnight, my wits already undone by terror, when the local TV station broke a special news story. Some sort of zombie doom coming our way, I figured. Instead, the story was about the failure of the potato crop.

The newscaster walked somberly through a field of potatoes reporting how few potatoes were growing on the bushes that season. He knelt and pushed aside the leaves to show the pendant potatoes growing two to a stem on the stalk. In good years, he said, there would be at least half a dozen on every branch.

I stared at the set. Weird, but something didn't seem right. It wasn't until the next morning that I thought, "Hey, potatoes don't grow above ground." The report had been an April Fool's prank. I hadn't realized the prank for what it was, perhaps because I still believed in the sanctity of the news as truth or because it was one o'clock in the morning, but also because potatoes are mysterious. Unlike squash or peas, you don't get to see potatoes growing. Even carrots and beets allow us at least a glimpse of their shoulders through the soil as they grow.

The mystery that surrounds the potato has given it a rather dodgy reputation at times. Until the late 1700s, many French refused to eat them thinking they caused leprosy. Further, in colonial Massachusetts, potatoes were considered the spoor of witches—which makes me laugh, imagining colonists stepping on spuds and complaining, "Ewww, witch poop!"

I also read that devout Scotch Presbyterians wouldn't eat potatoes because they weren't mentioned in the bible—a stance I imagine must have severely constrained their menu.

No such constraints at our house. When our eldest son, Jesse, was little, "potatoes and eggs" was his favorite meal. Enough potatoes in chicken potpie could make my carnivorous Sam and Louis happy with veggie potpie, and my famous green-chile chili wouldn't be right without diced potatoes adding their heft to the mix.

If I was going to win Louis and Sam over to eating out of the garden, I would have to grow potatoes on the Quarter Acre Farm. The good thing was, besides their culinary attraction, potatoes were reported to be easy to grow. Indeed, potatoes are so eager to proliferate, they even sprout in the refrigerator, a place you're specifically *not* trying to encourage them to be anything but an inert lump of starch.

Other people seemed to have no trouble growing the things. The trouble was, the few times I had taken a stab at potato raising, I'd met abject failure.

At my most creative, I'd planted potatoes in an inverted trash can, the bottom cut off. I heaped dirt in it as the vines grew with promising luxuriance, supposedly ensuring layers upon layers of meaty potatoes. I imagined eventually slipping the garbage can up off the cone of dirt and therein finding hundreds of potatoes for my efforts. The reality of it is, lush foliage does not mean lots of potatoes. Sam and I combed through the dirt and came up with hardly anything. The math? Two pounds of sprouted potatoes plus months of water and care resulted in a handful of marble-sized baby spuds.

Why, oh why couldn't I grow potatoes? Some guy in Lebanon had grown a *twenty-five-pound* potato. I wasn't expecting that, I just thought it would be nice to get a tuber that was bigger than a ping-pong ball.

Driving through the Central Valley in June, I was mocked by the thousands, maybe millions, of potato bags heaving full with spuds pulled from the pale soil. I knew those potato plants hadn't had the attention I'd lavished on my own. Why were those potatoes so eager to reproduce? More to the point, why weren't my potatoes doing it?

My mother grew potatoes. One of my sweetest childhood memories was of my mom making me homegrown baby potatoes and creamed peas for dinner on my birthday in early August. Come to think of it, I do only remember *baby* potatoes, not big ones . . . and those didn't come around much more often than my birthday. Perhaps my inability to grow potatoes was genetic.

But then I talked to a friend of mine who worked at the farmers' market (and was therefore privy to real farming advice), and I got an inkling that perhaps my problem wasn't so much a lack of potato-growing DNA as much as it was a lack of information. He said he was going to plant his garden potatoes when the farmers around Davis put their potatoes in the ground—in February.

My mind reeled. It is *cold* in February. I always planted my potatoes in the summer, not spring, and certainly not in the winter. But then I thought about the bags and bags of jumbo-sized potatoes already collected in the fields by June and decided I needed to educate myself.

The first step in my education was to master the vocabulary of growing potatoes. Whereas *chitting* is the process of exposing potatoes to warmth and light to encourage their eyes to sprout, *suberizing* is what happens when the potato seals off the cuts that come from being divided, or the wounds and skin damage acquired during harvest.

Both *haulms* and *shaws* refer to the potato leaves and stalks. *Round seed* is an uncut potato used for planting. *Seedpiece*, on the other hand, is a cut section of a potato with one or more eyes that is used for planting. *Seedpiece breakdown* refers to the seedpiece rotting due to waterlogged dirt and/or the potato not having been allowed to suberize.

Tubers were what I was aiming for—enlarged underground stems, the part of the potato plant that's edible.

As I familiarized myself with the world of the potato, I found that almost everything that I thought I knew about potatoes was wrong. Even though potatoes are related to tobacco and tomatoes, a family of plants that appreciate summer heat, my sense that potatoes were torrid-weather proliferators couldn't have been farther from the truth.

Instead, potatoes are a *cool season* crop. Not surprising to the people who know that potatoes first hailed from the Andes at an elevation of around 12,500 feet above sea level. The 8,000 years that the Peruvians have been eating potatoes have been put to good use. The International Potato Center in Lima maintains a tuber collection of over 4,500 types of potatoes. In the United States, however, over ninety percent of the potatoes we eat come from only twelve varieties.

While Ireland does not have a potato center, they are another famous lover of the potato and yet another cool-weather bastion. The difference between the height of summer and the depth of winter in Ireland can be a tiny thirty-degree difference in the temperature of the rain.
No matter where you hearken from, you can plant the round seed or suberized seed pieces of the potato when the ground temperature is a mere 45 degrees. Potatoes do best when the air temperatures are 60 to 75 degrees during the day and 45 to 55 degrees during the night.

No wonder my garbage can idea didn't work. Not only was it late June and 80 to 90 degrees during the day when I planted the potatoes in the garbage can (potato yields are highest when daytime temperatures are about 69 degrees), but the garbage can was a solarizing black on top of it. The temperature inside the Rubbermaid barrel must have been in baking range—certainly much higher than the 85 degree soil temperatures at which potatoes *stop* producing. Whoops.

I also believed that a potato needed lots of water initially to encourage the sprout and help the plant get a good start, just like seeds need to be kept moist in order to germinate. Instead, during the first stage of potato growth, the danger is of the seedpiece rotting from being too wet. This dooms the plant to failure since the seedpiece is the sole source of energy for the sprout until it emerges from the soil. Generally, although the dirt is damp when the potatoes are planted, *no* water is given for about two weeks until the green tip of the potato pokes out of the dirt. Whoops again.

In the second stage of growth, lasting from one to two months, the potato's vegetation forms and then (in some varieties but not all) it blooms. I thought that when a potato plant bloomed it was signaling that it was done with its work. After all, if a carrot or parsnip blooms, it means the plant is likely old and inedible beneath the ground. Instead, the blooming potato (or, for those varieties that don't bloom, the densely leafed potato) signals a time of tuber set and tuber initiation. While in the past I stopped watering at this point, this was actually the time when the potato needs the most water of all. Whoops three times.

Finally, the vines turn yellow and lose their leaves. When photosynthesis decreases, tuber growth naturally slows down and watering should be stopped. The tubers are left in the dry ground for two to three weeks, giving the potato skins time to toughen a bit before they are dug up.

Now that I was armed with knowledge, what I needed were seed potatoes. I bought some beautiful organic ones at the farmers' market. (The vendors at our farmers' market must grow what they sell, so buying locally grown potatoes meant they grew well in this area.) If you don't know your local potato grower, it is a good idea to buy seed potatoes from a source that can verify they are disease free and not inoculated with a substance (synthetic hormone) that inhibits sprouting.

I cut the largest potatoes into pieces that were no smaller than a golf ball, with at least two eyes. I allowed the pieces to suberize, or heal, which I now knew was done through the potato's formation of suberin (a waxy substance that functions to prevent water from penetrating the surface. Cork, interestingly, consists mainly of suberin).

I put the potatoes on the windowsill to "chit" (if you recall, chitting means to place in warm light to get the eyes to sprout). They quickly turned green, which is fine for a seed potato but is something you don't want to happen with your eating potatoes since the green indicates the presence of alkaloids (solanine and chaconine) in the skin, both of which are poisonous.

When February finally rolled sloooooowly and greyly around, I planted healthy seedpieces in the rich, well-draining soil in one of my raised beds.

Some years, of course, have colder, wetter conditions in February that might not be ideal for starting potatoes that early. Some places have heavier soils, which can facilitate rot. So how does one know?

It is almost impossible to find every potato when you dig up the beds. There are always a few that get left in the dirt. I expect that they will rot, but they often come up the next year as volunteers. They are excellent markers. When I see the first leaves of the volunteers, I know that the time to plant new potatoes is *now* (though not in the same place).

In subsequent years of growing potatoes, it is important to change the location of your potato plants in order to sidestep the possibility of plant diseases. Potatoes are as beloved by fungi as they are by people. Early blight, late blight, wilt, black scurf, *Rhizoctonia canker*, and silver scurf, to name a few types of spud-crazy fungi, would all love to have their way with your potatoes before you get a chance to shred them into hash. These fungi hang out in the soil and if you plant where they've got a start (from a previous season's planting), they will attack their host plants with a vengeance. Suffice to say, it won't be pretty. This is the same reason you don't want to plant tomatoes, eggplant, or even tobacco in the same area either; they are all vulnerable to the same funguses and diseases.

My second year of potatoes seemed to be doing fine. I hoped I'd got the timing right by planting early. I followed up the early planting by watering as recommended. The leaves of the potatoes grew luxuriant and tall, and then the plant blossomed. Of course, I knew better than to believe that meant bushels of potatoes were burgeoning out of sight. I held my expectations in check and continued watering as the blossoming continued. When the leaves yellowed I withheld water . . . and waited, allowing the potatoes that might have grown (or might not have) to toughen. I must admit, the two weeks that followed were suspenseful indeed . . . I may even have dug around just a bit hoping to come across a small patch of witch spoor, but I was disappointed. Had I failed again?

When the toughening period ended, I took out my pitchfork (using a pitchfork cuts down the likelihood that you will slice into a potato) and turned over the earth. The bad news was that I didn't get a twenty-five-pound potato, but I *did* get more than twenty-five pounds of potatoes in total. And a good number of them were *fist-sized* tubers. This, for me, was practically a miracle.

In the meantime, my hens had been churning out eggs. And so for our personal potato day celebration, we made Jesse's favorite childhood meal.

Potatoes and Eggs

For most of Jesse's childhood, potatoes and eggs was a weekly dinner. It started out as a cost-saving meal but became a dinner of choice, especially for a skinny freckled child who could put away more potatoes and eggs than seemed anatomically possible.

I have to say, cooking potatoes was a job fraught with difficulties for me. The sliced potatoes would get gummy, the eggs would be like rubber, or the potatoes would be crunchy. One would think that coming from the meat and potatoes family of my childhood I would be able to fry up some spuds blindfolded.

No matter the problems I had with them, Jesse ate each and every permutation of potatoes and eggs, leading me to believe he would eat *anything* (I found that this wasn't true on the day we ran out of tomato sauce and I substituted ketchup on Jesse's pizza).

I never added ketchup to eggs, but I did eventually discover the best way to make potatoes and eggs—at least for me.

Ingredients:

- 4 potatoes
- 6 eggs
- 1 cup chopped green onions (or more, depending on your taste)
- salt and pepper to taste
- 1 dash cayenne (optional)
- 1 healthy glug of olive oil

1. Cut the raw potatoes (as many or as few as you'd like, really) into half-inch cubes, toss with copious amounts of sliced green onions and a goodly amount of salt (potatoes beg for salt), a dash of pepper, and enough olive oil to coat the mixture.

2. Either spread the mixture on a cookie sheet (use a Silpat baking mat or parchment paper to make cleanup easier) and roast the potatoes in a pre-heated 400 degree oven, or toss them into a frying pan and sauté them on the stovetop, which has the added advantage of one less dish to clean.

3. Beat the eggs with a splash of milk until foamy.

4. When the potatoes have browned on a couple of sides, arrange them evenly in the hot skillet and pour the egg mixture over them. You want to treat the eggs gently.

5. Turn down the heat and cook the potatoes and eggs a few minutes on a medium-low burner, then stick the skillet under the broiler on low until the eggs, though cooked, are still quite moist.

6. Remove skillet from broiler, let sit for a few minutes, and season with salt, pepper, and/or cayenne before serving (for breakfast burritos, serve with warm tortillas and salsa).

Alotta Frittata

Potatoes and eggs continued to be one of my favored dishes when I started the Quarter-Acre Farm project, especially when the fowl hit their (re)productive strides. The two chickens would lay two eggs a day, the duck one every other day, and while Jeannette was responsible for only about two dozen a year, they were enormous eggs. (Sometimes people ask us if we aren't tempted to let Jeannette and Goosteau hatch their eggs. While I admit a gosling is about the most endearing baby animal on the planet, the idea of more Goosteaus and Jeannettes rampaging across the Quarter-Acre Farm is enough to make me dizzy with dread.)

However, as the potatoes proved to be a problem (ahem) for me to grow, I started sneaking other vegetables into the potatoes and eggs mix: pea shoots, chard, broccoli, fava greens, sugar peas, spinach, sun-dried tomatoes, green onions, and garlic to name a few—sometimes even leaving out the potatoes altogether and adding different kinds of cheeses to the egg mixture. To reflect these fancy-pants changes, we started using the fancy-pants word for the resulting dish: frittata. Who wouldn't love frittata when it rhymes so well with alotta? (Oh, imagine eating alotta *ricotta* frittata!) Okay, my boys don't think it's as funny as I do. However, they still love frittatas.

Ingredients:

- 6 to 12 cups chopped vegetables (½ to 1 cup per egg)
- 12 eggs
- 1 cup shredded Romano cheese (or other cheese of choice)
- milk (as needed)
- salt and pepper to taste
- a dash of seasonings (whatever you prefer—thyme, tarragon, rosemary, cayenne, etc.)

1. I use a lot of vegetables in our frittatas. To me, the eggs in the best frittatas are less of a main component than a flavorful "glue" to keep all the greens stuck together. And one key to a good frittata is to cook whatever vegetables you are using *previous* to adding the egg. If you are sautéing them in the frittata pan, cook them in the order of time they take to cook. That is, you don't want to throw the chard into the pan at the same time as the broccoli florettes. The chard will be over-done or the broccoli won't be done enough. Either start with the florettes and cook until almost tender before adding, say, snap peas; or blanch/roast/steam the heavy stuff like broccoli, cauliflower, or potatoes ahead of time.

2. Beat the eggs and milk just until the yolks and whites are barely incorporated. I treat my egg "glue" with great gentleness so that the egg component doesn't actually resemble glue (or rubber) when I eat it.

3. Fold in the cheese and any other seasonings you might want to use (I use salt and pepper of course, but also maybe some tarragon, or some rosemary or thyme).

4. Pour the egg mixture over the cooked vegetables in the hot skillet and wait a couple of minutes (with the burner turned to low).

5. Put the pan under the broiler set to low. Let cook for the time it takes for the eggs to set (approximately 5-15 minutes depending on the size of your pan and the depth of your frittata). As with the eggs and potatoes, the frittata should appear slightly underdone when you pull it from the oven because the eggs will continue to cook for a few minutes once out of the hot stove.

6. Let the frittata cool a bit before serving, or let it cool a lot, because the dish is delicious at room temperature.

Note: Frittata makes a wonderful picnic entree, so the next time you are heading out to a public concert to listen to, say, a *cantata*, or you're going to the river where you'll perhaps see a *regatta*, you know what you need to make *alotta* of.

MAGICAL FRUIT

"I like refried beans. That's why I wanna try fried beans, because maybe they're just as good and we're just wasting time."
—MITCH HEDBERG

If potatoes are good stick-to-your-ribs food, then their cousins in the basic fill-you-up food genre are beans.

Why grow beans? You can buy enough legumes to fill a city's worth of burritos for less than it costs one person to eat at the French Laundry. Further, they require a lot of steps to grow and harvest. Unlike say, zucchini or tomatoes, you have to not only grow and pick the beans, but also dry them, remove them from their pods, and thresh and clean them, all *before* preparing them to eat. Taking these vegetables from a naked seed that you poke into the soil all the way through its growth cycle to become yet *another* naked seed, which you then poke into a stockpot (hopefully with quite a few of its brothers), is no small task.

If I hadn't decided to grow 75 percent of my food in my yard, and I hadn't worried that buying beans might have meant giving up a wedge of Mt. Tam cheese, I wouldn't have used my garden space for something I could buy for pennies. And what a shame that would have been.

As it was, I almost didn't get to discover what a treat homegrown beans actually are. I planted my beans in a bed that was apparently slated for the construction of a sow bug city-state. As my beans grew, the sow bug citizens munched down on every bit of pale tender shoot that poked out of the earth. Yes I know sow bugs (a.k.a. roly polies) aren't supposed to eat living plants. They are supposed to be the vultures of the garden world, chowing down on the dead. Apparently some of the crustacean-looking fellows like both. Apparently *a lot* of them like both.

After the lot of them had consumed over five dollars of bean seed, I wasn't keen on buying more seed packets. But then, standing at the organic bulk bins at the co-op, I stared at the lovely array of beans ready to be made into stews. These beans were *much* less expensive than the packets I bought at the nursery. Beans are beans, right? They were organic and so had not been sprayed with any inhibitory hormones. At a fraction of the cost, I could risk replanting with these.

I bought a small amount of organic cranberry beans, pinto beans, and turtle beans. Crossing my fingers, I went home, chose a bed *away* from the burgeoning sow bug metropolis, and planted the beans.

All three types sprouted without any problem, grew like a dream, and produced a lot of bean pods. When the pods dried, I picked them and laid them in a single layer on a tray in the house for a day or so to make sure they were well dehydrated. Many of the beans sprung from their pods as I was picking them, so to keep from having to ferret the beans out of the dirt, I got in the habit of placing a tray under the bush I was harvesting.

When the beans seemed dry enough (a fully dried bean is one hard enough that you don't leave a print when you press a fingernail into the skin), it was time to shell them.

Methods varied. I read about one guy who separated his beans from their dried pods by putting them in a bag, which he whacked on the ground for a while. I'd worry a little about breaking the beans, but perhaps he was whacking gently.

I went for a more subdued method, though likely not as much fun. I put the pods in a box and scrunched them with my hands until they crackled open. I scrunched and scrunched and threw away the large pieces of empty pods until I was left with a pile of beans and a huge amount of chaff.

To get rid of the chaff, I took my beans outside in a dishcloth hammocked between my two hands and gently tossed the mixture up and down, letting the breeze blow the chaff away. This worked to some extent, but the breeze wasn't quite strong enough to take care of all of it. Then I tried blowing into the chaff/bean mix as I tossed it. But very quickly I wavered dizzily on the verge of hyperventilation. My tossing became so erratic that I repeatedly had to stop and pick up beans I'd accidentally flung onto the ground. No wonder.

With the next batch of beans, I figured out a way to blow the chaff away without the risk of blacking out mid-procedure. I turned on a fan and placed a container on the ground beside it. As I poured the mixture into the container, the fan blew the chaff away from the stream of beans, which fell cleanly into the container. I finished the job on my feet.

I stored my beans in a glass jar. To prevent molding, I tossed in one of those packets that come in vitamin jars.

When it came time to cook the beans, I made a pot of my famous green-chile chili using my homegrown cranberry beans. The beans were delicious—tender, with a smooth texture, having what would be called "tooth" if they were pasta. Sam asked what kind of beans were in it. They were really *good*. Louis concurred.

Were homegrown beans that much better, or was it merely a "grew it myself" pride that colored our perception of the legumes? I decided to test our perceptions. I made the chili again the next week with store-bought beans. It was usual good, but not *good* good. Why would this be?

If beans are less than six months old, they may not even require soaking before cooking. They plump up quickly. Commercially produced beans are usually much older than six months by the time you purchase them in the store, often as far as three years from their harvest. (One of the possible drawbacks to using them as seed.) The longer a bean has been stored, the more likely it is to absorb odors, and to change colors and taste.

Commercial beans are also processed by machinery. This can be hard on a poor little bean. If the beans are even a little too dry, they are subject to cracking, splitting, and checkering, especially under the duress of a machine's hard surfaces. If a bean's skin is damaged, it cooks differently and is more likely to become mealy in the pot.

If the beans aren't quite dry enough at harvest, they are prone to molding. Even in a metal storage facility, beans that touch the walls will sweat if aeration is not just right.

I am always ready to make a change if it will make something taste better. But this isn't the only reason to grow your own beans. Consider this: commercial beans are planted, cut, and threshed by tractors, then trucked to a processor where they are machine washed, machine milled, polished, and poured by machines into bulk bags. The bags are trucked to processing plants, packaged into smaller bags (machine-made plastic) for the consumer, and then *those* bags are trucked out to the grocery outlets, to which the consumer drives in order to purchase a measure of legumes for stew. That's a lot of petroleum product going into those beans.

Further, commercial beans are usually subjected to two to three fungicidal treatments before harvest. When the farmer sees that most of the beans in the field are close to harvest, an herbicide such as Roundup is applied to the leaves to kill the plants so that the beans will be drier when they are harvested a number of days thereafter. As a result, however, the beans may carry traces of the herbicide in their fruit.

If that isn't enough to make you go running for the trowel, here's more good news. Beans are recommended for first-time gardeners because they are *super easy to grow*. So easy, in fact, that it seems everyone grew a bean plant as a science experiment in grade school. Including me. When I was ten years old, I got a third-place ribbon in a science fair for testing the effect of feeding milk to bean plants instead of just water. There may have only been three science fair entries in my age group, come to think of it, but the point is that my room smelled like soured cream for the entire month I grew beans. If beans will grow with rancid dairy products mucking up their environment, you know they will grow for you.

While growing your beans will be easy, there are a number of difficult decisions to be made before digging in. The first decision will be whether you'd like to grow snap beans, shelling beans, or dried beans. That is, do you want to eat fresh beans *in* the pod, fresh beans *out* of the pod, or *dried* beans out of the pod?

Further complicating matters is that beans come in "bush varieties" and "pole varieties." Bush varieties, on the plus side, don't need support and often produce their fruit earlier than pole beans. However, they often don't produce as long, and the beans get dirtier being that close to the ground. Pole beans require staking but they produce their beans for a longer time, and the beans are often straighter and cleaner since they are developing in the penthouse suite rather than ground floor.

The most important choice, however, is one that not everyone realizes is a choice at all. At least *I* wasn't aware of it. While I understood beans came in different colors, it seemed to be an aesthetic difference, and choosing between them was akin to picking the green iPod over the hot-pink one. Beans taste like . . . beans, after all.

Turns out, beans have flavors as varied as those of cheese. For instance, while pintos are said to have an earthy flavor and a mushier texture, cranberry beans are more delicate, tasting nutty. Anasazi beans are sweeter. French green lentils are peppery in taste, and garbanzos have a walnutty-chestnutty aspect. Favas are characterized as sweet-earthy, flageolet as creamy. Turtle beans have a strong, almost mushroom-like flavor and floury texture, and pigeon peas (ancient beans that have been found in Egyptian tombs) have the reputation of being slightly narcotic.

How to choose? Perhaps the best way is by recipe—what do you like to eat? Greek giant oven-baked beans? Go for butter beans. Black beans are indispensable if you make your own veggie burgers. Tuscan bean soup calls for kidney beans, and cannelloni and crostini go together like, well, cannelloni and crostini. A fan of Japanese kuri yokan? Grow azuki beans. My favorite soup is chickpea with orzo and rosemary, and mung beans added to chopped beets and onion, vinegar and honey is pretty wonderful too. Red beans stand up well to meat—such as sausages or in chili with chicken. Fava beans tossed with olive oil and lemon juice are pretty much a perfect meal.

In other words, set aside a good part of your garden for beans. You'll want to try bean bourguignon, to cook up some cassoulet, and to not forget three-bean salad, green bean casserole, fabada asturiana (Spanish bean stew), Great Northern beans with ham, beans in garlic sauce, black beans and mango, and even black bean brownies.

Green-Chile Chili

There are more arguments about the length of time required to soak beans than there are about the merits of one political party versus the other, and neither are very likely to be resolved. The reasons, at least with the bean debate, are clear: soaking time depends on how dry the beans are, how old, what kind of beans you are using, how big those beans are, and even the preferred texture of bean dishes. I'll tell you what I do with my dried-this-season beans, but I recommend you experiment on your own, read up on it, call your mother, or all of the above

Another point of contention with beans is the issue of gas. When soaked, beans release complex carbohydrates (raffinose sugars) that are *not* broken down in digestion, hanging out instead in the large intestine, fermenting. Generally I'm all in favor of fermentation, but not so much the intestinal kind. (When Jesse was young he used to *refuse* to eat beans on a school night. If I forgot and served them, he'd glower and make himself a peanut butter and jelly sandwich instead.) People try all sorts of things to get around the problem, from throwing away several rounds of soaking water or taking anti-gas tablets available at drug stores, to timing their bean consumption around, say, school holidays.

Once a person eats more fruits and vegetables, however, their systems adjust to being bean friendly. Now that we eat out of the garden most nights, we don't experience the "problem beans are famous for." A revelation appreciated by all, I'm sure.

There is yet another bone of contention in the world of bean cookery—the salt and tomato (or acid) issue. You can find plenty of legume aficionados who will insist that salt and/or tomatoes will keep the beans from softening correctly. What I have deduced from reading scientific sources on "to salt and tomato your beans or not to salt and tomato" is that salt will merely make things saltier, and the acid in the tomatoes keeps the skins intact. I can imagine how the acid effect would seem (or even directly affect) a longer cooking time if you like your beans mushier (broken skins will make that happen), but I figure one should put the salt and tomatoes in whenever they wish, as far as cooking time is concerned.

One trick that does make a difference for me is making sure that once the beans are up to boil, I turn the beans down *low*. If I ever mess up this dish it's because I believe I can speed things up by increasing the heat, but then the liquid boils away, and if I don't actually *burn* the beans (which is usually the case), I end up with beans mushier than I care for.

Ingredients:

- 2 carrots
- 2 stalks of celery
- 2 cups of green chile (roasted, peeled, seeded, and chopped)
- 2 cups of chopped tomatoes
- 4 large potatoes cut into one-inch cubes (I wish it were just 2 potatoes to keep up with the 2 "theme," but they would have to be *humungous* spuds)
- 2 cups of dried beans
- Salt to taste

1. Rinse the beans, removing any chaff or detritus.

2. Cover the cleaned beans in water and let them sit. I usually do this around lunch and then unfortunately forget about the whole thing until an hour or two before dinner—or, more likely, just about the time everyone's asking if dinner's almost ready.

3. Pour the beans into a colander and let them drain. I usually take this opportunity to dice the carrots, onions, and celery into small pieces.

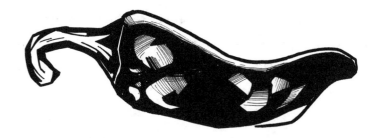

4. Saute the vegetables in olive oil in a stew pot until the onions are translucent.

5. Add the soaked beans and green chile (which is usually a frozen brick of green chile I grew and roasted in the summer), the tomatoes, and the salt to the pot and top it up with either water or stock until there is 2 to 3 inches of liquid over the top of the beans.

6. Bring the whole thing to a boil then turn the temperature down so that the beans are *barely* at a simmer. Cook for approximately 3 hours or until the beans are tender. I try to keep an eye on it, adding water as needed.

7. Throw in the potatoes during the last half hour.

By the time my homegrown beans are tender, the potatoes are usually done as well and the stew has thickened nicely.

If I've remembered to start the stew in good time, we usually eat it the same night. If I haven't, then we have grilled cheese sandwiches (I call them "panini" to make it sound like I'm on top of things, after all). When the stew is finished, I refrigerate it to eat the next night.

That's for the best, really. If you want the very best green-chile chili *ever*, you will steel yourself to wait to eat it for dinner the next day. Green chile stew *always* tastes better the second day. Serve with hot sauce and hot tortillas.

WEEDS

"What would the world be, once bereft of wet and wilderness?
Let them be left, Oh let them be left, wilderness and wet;
Long live the weeds and the wilderness yet."
—GERALD MANLEY HOPKINS

My sister, Summer, was not only more daring than I but more beautiful. I had a round face, distinctly un-soulful eyes, and no desire to call attention to those facts by doing what Summer did the year she turned sixteen—dye her hair.

Summer came into my room post dye-job, her hair so audaciously dark and free of highlights it looked as if she had a shag-shaped black hole where her auburn hair had once been. She asked if I could tell that she had colored her hair. I choked out, "Yeah!" both writhing with the thrill of the coming *hell-to-pay* that for once had nothing to do with me, and also mourning for the sister who would soon be taken from me at my mother's hand.

In my family, teenager plus hair dye equaled prodigious amounts of weeding time. Thirty some years later, my sister is, I believe, still in hard labor in my parents' backyard, wrenching dandelions and bind-weed from the rocky soil.

When my kids hit the age of hair dye, Jesse begged me to let him change the color of his mop. I said certainly not—even though by then a kid changing his hair to Barbie doll black, or purple and orange stripes, for that matter, was hardly unusual. When my friends asked me if I really thought it so wrong, I scoffed, "Of course not. But there's work to be done!"

My kids also grew up righting their wrongs in the garden, which worked out pretty well—for me at least. I wouldn't go so far to say that I *hoped* they would misbehave, but it did make their transgressions so much easier to take when I knew their failure to turn in homework, their missed curfew, or the smell of tobacco on their clothes was going to translate into a weed-free garden to salve the trauma to their long-suffering mother.

Unfortunately, Sam caught on to my plan and has not even *approached* a bottle of hair dye.

When I started working the quarter acre, weeds seemed to be something I was truly gifted with growing. For every bean I managed to germinate, a hundred weeds sprouted from the soil. I was watering more Bermuda grass than beets and pulling more dandelions than carrots. By the time August came, a verdant porridge of weedage abounded, and I was beside myself. But I had a plan.

On the morning of August 4, I put a sign in my front yard that said, "It's my birthday. Help me weed!" I fantasized that my neighbors would walk by, chuckle, then say in a folksy tone reminiscent of Jimmy Stewart, "Well, now, I've got ten minutes, how 'bout I pull this patch of Bermuda grass for you?"

Strangers would then stop, marvel at all the neighbors pitching in like a barn was being raised, and they too would put their hand to yanking bindweed. Before I knew it, the Quarter-Acre Farm would be . . . pristine. Not a weed in evidence. Tamed.

Instead, the first thing that happened was that Sam read the sign and decided I was trying to humiliate him to death. And that was pretty much the only thing that happened. No one stopped by to help. Our street was as deserted as Tombstone on the day the Clantons came to town. I imagined my neighbors peering from behind their curtains, reading the sign, and shouting to their families, "Get back, she'll see you!"

Finally, in the late afternoon, the sweet boy next door showed up with a bouquet of flowers he had picked to wish me happy birthday. I exclaimed over the flowers then asked Daniel if he had seen the sign in the front yard. He squirmed. "Yee-es." I asked him if he'd like to be the first one to help, and before he could bolt I pointed to a strand of bindweed at his feet.

Really, it was a *symbolic gesture*. I didn't make him weed, not really. But still, Louis and Sam couldn't believe I had coerced the nice kid next door into doing my dirty work. I couldn't believe they couldn't believe it. That's the kind of thing you have to do when weeds are the problem.

Weeds thrive in disturbed soil. So while I was digging out grass and making hills and setting up new beds, I was turning a huge number of seeds into the dirt that I had so very carefully added amendments to so that the beds would be fertile. Then I very nicely watered it. I made the conditions *perfect* for plants, and as E.J. Salisbury pointed out in 1935, a weed is merely a plant out of place.

The worst "plant out of place" that I struggled with was bindweed. Bindweed is also commonly known as wild morning glory, or creeping Jenny, and was the first weed to be recognized as a *national menace* by the U.S. Department of Agriculture. I had been careful never to let the bindweed go to seed—so where was all the bindweed coming from? Turns out, bindweed seeds can survive for more than *twenty-five years* before germinating. Some of the seeds that were coming up in my beds may have come to fruition back when my sixteen-year-old sister was deciding between coloring her hair Parisian Onyx or Ebony Night.

If that wasn't bad enough, bindweed doesn't need to rely on seeds to proliferate. In one laboratory test plot, single bindweed, six months after germination, produced 197 vertical roots for a total count of 788 feet of roots. Add to that 34 horizontal roots on which there were 144 new shoot buds, *each of which is capable of becoming a new plant*. Weeds are vigorous. They are *crafty*, doing things like groutweed does, entangling its roots among those of desirable plants. They are pushy, like Broom, which grows so dense it doesn't allow any other plants to grow with it. They, like myrtle spurge, may be able to project their seeds many feet from the parent plant; or may, like purple loosestrife, produce three million seeds per plant. Weeds are very successful, and they were certainly winning in my garden.

As I looked around my weed-riven yard, I contemplated how easy it would be to take a quick trip to the hardware store, purchase a gallon of some herbicide labeled with a cheerful picture of a weed-free planet, and eliminate the throttle of noxious plants in my garden, once and for all. I was sorely, sorely tempted. But to steel myself, I took down a book on my shelf that the kids gave me for Christmas one year.

It is a textbook on weed control written in 1942 by three men at the nascent California Experimental Station here in Davis. It has a wealth of intriguing information within the yellowing pages. Reading it, I learned it takes 368 pounds of water to create one pound of dry corn matter, while it takes 948 pounds of water to create a dry pound of ragweed. (This fact may give you a hint about why your vegetable plants languish in a weedy bed.) Yet the truly sobering information concerns the chemical regulation of weeds.

The photographs in the book look familiar: the flat dry fields, creek edges, distant hills—there is a picture of a fenced field with an area cleared for planting. The old photograph was taken a few years before our house was built, and it is not beyond conjecture that the photograph is of the land on which our house would eventually be built.

Underneath the black and white photograph, it says the arid-looking landscape is a sterilization plot *seven years* after treatment with arsenic trioxide. The vegetation was only just starting to creep back onto the sterilized earth. This image was meant as a celebration of the chemical power deployed on it; a celebration that did not last.

Today I wonder how deeply the arsenic percolated and if it rises with the tunneling of ants and the reach of deep roots. Likely not, or so I hope. But I know the desire to believe in the easy chemical fix continues. Obviously I shared it myself.

I decided to leave the herbicides at the store, though every lazy bone in my body moaned at the thought of the hours of weeding ahead of me. There had to be a better way.

I once had high hopes that the geese would be of some use. Goosteau is of the goose breed called Chinese weeder, and we do call Jeannette the constant gardener due to her penchant for trimming plants. However, she resembles less an English lady shaping privet than Morticia Adams at work with lopping shears. I had a luxuriant four-and-a-half-foot-tall artichoke plant that Jeannette decided to prune. At day's end, I found her standing next to a naked stalk surrounded by a pile of clipped leaves. It was not an isolated incident. Jeannette will snip snip snip at anything her snake-like neck can hoist her serrated bill up to. She is not so much a weeder as a menace in the garden.

As for Goosteau, I read that you prime the Chinese weeder goslings to actually weed by feeding them only the weeds you want them to pull from your garden. They supposedly will grow up with a taste for burdock or spurge or bindweed. Did it work? If you had a field full of weeds and turned geese into it, I'm sure they would do a pretty good job in getting rid of the stuff. But if you have a yard full of tender peas, lettuce, *and* bindweed, and a goose gets loose in it, the peas and lettuce will assuredly not survive.

Additionally, whatever doesn't get eaten will likely be mashed by the geese's big feet. A study on vertebrate herbivores as biological control found that trampling by geese led to a 47 percent spruce seedling mortality. The irony was that the researchers chose spruce seedling as a prototype crop that would be *unpalatable* to geese. I'll bet Jeannette would have pruned the other 53 percent anyway.

With chemicals, geese, and my Tom Sawyeresque get-the-neighbors-to-do-it-for-me method all nixed as a reliable method of weed control, and Sam selfishly behaving himself so that I could not punish him with chores, I was left with hand weeding all by myself. I still have not found another solution. I'm sorry. Boy, am I sorry.

The only thing to do if you hate weeds and can't figure out a good way to kill them is to make sure they don't grow in the first place. That sounds like the advice given on how to get rich: pick wealthy parents. But there is a way, and the way is called mulch. Mulch has proven to be one of the most effective ways to control weeds.

Just the word mulch makes Louis wince. We so often have a pile of chipped tree trimmings from arborists working in the neighborhood that Louis is almost as famous in his University department for barrowing prodigious amounts of it into the backyard as he is for writing his award-winning books. "Moving any mulch today, professor?" someone will ask jovially, and Louis will give me the look.

Our neighbor Millicent walked across the street one day, years after we had moved in, and asked to look in our backyard. I said of course and took her back to see the little fruit trees we had planted there. She looked around the yard with an expression of profound disappointment and said, "I've watched you take so many chips into the backyard, I thought it would be ten feet deep with it."

At any given time in our yard there is between four and eighteen inches of mulch on the ground, in and around our gardening beds, and under the fruit trees. Before you know it, eighteen inches of mulch breaks down into four inches then into two, and then it's time to add more if you wish the mulch to be an efficient weed barrier.

Why? Most seeds need light to germinate, and apparently light can filter through dirt and mulch. It usually takes about four inches or more of mulch to keep seeds from germinating. (This is one of the reasons you don't want to mulch beds with newly planted seeds you *want* to grow. Save mulching until your plants are tall enough to rise well above the surface of the soil.)

Those are just the seeds, however. Four inches of mulch isn't going to keep a strand of Bermuda grass down. In areas with lots of unwanted weedy growth, I put down cardboard first, then top it with mulch. Lots of it. I'm going for eighteen inches of depth at that point and as a result, I find myself riding my bike around the neighborhood listening for the roar of chainsaws and stump grinders that signal a possible mulch haul.

I have to admit, even with eighteen inches of mulch on my path-ways, I still get the dreaded bindweed. However, when bindweed surfaces in mulch, it is so much easier to yank up. Yes, some of it comes back because of the plant's superpower of regrowth from a tiny section of root, but I keep putting mulch over the top of it, keep yanking it, and I have made great headway in slowing the noxious plant's colonial fervor.

Furthermore, the weeds that are not as pernicious as bindweed are easily yanked from mulch, and then much more easily smothered by repeated application of another layer of mulch. If most weeds are absent from your garden, it will make the battle waged on the ones that do remain a little easier to bear.

Mulching isn't perfect . . . Louis would be the first to tell anyone that all that shoveling, barrowing, and raking is hard on a guy's back. And I will warn a prospective mulcher that mulch is a hiding place for voracious sowbugs, snails, and slugs. That said, there are a lot more reasons to mulch than just weed control, which will make muscle aches and snail vigilance seem a small price to pay for the following benefits:

Mulch reduces moisture loss in soils up to twenty-five percent. (Just the amount of time saved in watering will pay for the time spent spreading mulch!)

Mulch keeps the soil warmer in the winter and cooler in the summer, allowing plants to put more energy into fruiting than into driving their roots into deeper cooler areas.

With the tempering effects of mulch, your vegetables will produce longer. Mulching also impedes some loss of nitrogen because it keeps the direct sun off the soil's surface. (Making up for some of the nitrogen loss that mulch breakdown can cause.)

Mulch improves the soil, encouraging microorganisms and earthworms to live in your garden's dirt. The minerals and organic matter that are gradually released from decaying mulch replace the nutrients used by growing plants.

Mulch improves water retention by breaking down clay soil and improving the holding capacity of sandy soil. It can help keep water and mud from being splashed on leaf surfaces, which can cause soilborne diseases.

All in all, mulching is such a good idea, and even Louis has come around to admitting its strengths. He has even, on a sunny day while enjoying a long cold drink (instead of having to weed or to water), offered as a Quarter-Acre Farm credo, "Mulch the planet!"

Indeed.

Purslane Salad

More often than not, purslane is considered a weed. As such, it is often overlooked as both a culinary delight and a nutritional powerhouse (rich in fiber, vitamins, minerals, and more omega-3 fatty acids than many fish oils). Purslane has a sprightly taste, grows like crazy in the hottest part of the year, and is a lovely bright-green color—all of which make it a perfect salad base, especially when tossed with equal amounts tomato.

Ingredients:

- 2 cups de-stemmed purslane
- 2 cups deseeded and diced tomatoes
- 1 cup sorrel
- ½ red onion
- extra-virgin olive oil

- 2 TB lemon juice
- 1 cup crumbled feta
- salt and pepper to taste

The combination of the sweet-tasting tomatoes and the peppery purslane can only be made better by adding lemony sorrel that is de-stemmed and cut into thin strips, which is also growing great guns at the same time as the purslane and tomatoes. (It doesn't take much brainpower to figure this salad out. Mother Nature is doing it for us.) The only thing missing now is perhaps a spicy crunch—which is perfectly fulfilled by adding half an onion cut into thin rings. Toss it with a drizzle of really good extra-virgin olive oil, fresh-squeezed lemon juice, and crumbled feta, then sprinkle with salt and pepper to taste, and serve.

WHEN GOOD BUGS GO BAD

*"Big fleas have little fleas
Upon their back to bite 'em;
Little fleas have smaller fleas,
And so on, ad infinitum."*
—ANONYMOUS

Once upon a time (late 1930s), there was a Swiss scientist named Paul Muller, the son of a railway man and a future Nobel Prize winner, who discovered the insecticidal properties of a substance known as DDT (dichlorodiphenyltrichloroethane). This discovery, along with that of the insecticidal properties of organophosphates by German and Allied scientists who were actually trying to create new and improved nerve gasses, birthed the pesticide era.

No matter that DDT had a disastrous effect on not only insects but also fish and (most famously) birds of prey due to the bioamplification of the substance, DDT supporters believed so strongly in its low toxicity to humans that they publicly ate the powder and showed no harmful effects. The nerve poisons, on the other hand, were not only effective insect killers, but they were also virtually as nasty to humans as originally intended. In spite of this, these chemicals were thought to herald a golden

era free from the quadrillion insects that plagued humans by spreading disease, consuming crops, and otherwise irritating us on picnics.

Pesticides *did* make inroads along those lines, saving millions of lives from the ravages of mosquito-borne malaria, for one. Summer parties were protected from creepy crawlies with applications of Knox-Out, and fruit maintained unblemished skin after being dusted with Sevin to deter pests (which wasn't so good for the orchard workers either, to put it mildly).

But we do worry, if over the wrong things. The more we fought back bugs, the less tolerance we had for them—an intolerance that is nurtured today by chemical and extermination companies, to amazing effect. Pesticide use has increased fifty-fold since 1950, and it is likely to continue. Look at Pestworld.com, the National Pest Management Association website, where you will find fun facts for kids such as that a cockroach can run 30 mph, 14,000 people a year are bitten by rats, termites eat nonstop 24/7, and fleas have killed more people than all world wars combined. Who wouldn't be afraid of such a speedy, hungry, vicious, deadly horde?

It seems a pretty transparent bid for extermination contracts, but I am the last person to pretend I don't understand the panic that insects can cause in people.

When I was four years old, I slept more often on the carpet outside my parents' bedroom than in my own bed, beset with nightmares about bugs in my room. At five I fell down the stairs because I panicked over a beetle on my skirt, and in first grade I froze in terror when a wasp landed on my cheek and crawled up my nose. Luckily, the wasp backed out (literally), and I was famous at Sundance Elementary—but not in a good way.

And so it went until I was a teenager picking blackberries at the ranch when what I had taken for the tickle of branches on my leg was actually a spider the size of a cantaloupe clinging to my bare thigh. It was then that I squandered the remainder of my lifetime allotment of insect terror in one terrific scream.

Historically, that scream for the pesticide era was Rachel Carson and her 1962 book, *Silent Spring* (ha ha, how ironic!), in which she revealed that pesticides were causing environmental catastrophe. Monsanto reacted by publishing a response to Carson's book that described a world laid to waste by insects, famine, and disease because pesticides had been banned. DDT could be purchased at the local hardware store until 1972, and we are now more likely to call the exterminator at the summer hum of insects than we are to consider it music.

When our kids were young, I made up for my early distaste for the bug world with a vengeance—carefully ferrying beetles that blundered into the house back to the yard, scanning firewood for earwigs before throwing it into the fire. When the kids went through their bug-collecting stage, I helped them save drowned insects in pool filters rather than kill live ones, explaining that all insects had their place in the world. Even wasps, much like the one that crawled up Mama's nose, were the sole pollinators of one of our favorite foods—figs.

Further, I am now very spider-friendly. (You would guess this if you came to the house and looked into the cobwebby corners.) Louis, Sam, Jesse, and I watched one wolf spider for months, in the window, at the ceiling, between bookshelf and wall, capturing gnats and even laying an egg case that looked as though it had been upholstered in a Q-tip. When the eggs hatched we were shocked to find thousands of spiders the size of punctuation points all over the white walls. Within half an hour, however, they had all, eerily, disappeared. But when I lifted the edge of a painting from the wall, dozens peeked out from underneath. The day after that they were not even to be seen in corners. I suspect cannibalism.

However, I am not *fully* enlightened. I recognize there are reasons that DDT was such a hit. Mosquitoes and the threat of West Nile disease worry me, cockroaches make me shudder, and when the ants try to move inside when the rains come each year, I lose all sympathy. When I began competing with insects for food crops in my own garden, it added another layer of complexity to my feelings toward bugs.

Around the world, insects are responsible for eating 10 percent of our food crops each year (though I would like to see a statistic on how much of our fruits and vegetables are wasted, rotting in the crisper section of our refrigerators or shriveling on the counter, before I get too bent out of shape about *that*). Insects, in any case, were certainly taking their share of my personal crop at the Quarter-Acre farm.

I didn't want to use pesticides in the garden. I liked eating things off the vine too much for that, and I envisioned myself in Sleeping Beauty mode tra-la-la-ing a duet with bluebirds and butterflies as I danced lightly through nature. I would foreswear any but organic means to convince the insects to leave my yard in peace. If I couldn't use Sevin or Raid, however, I wasn't sure what those means would be.

It was second nature for our parents, even grandparents, to put 100 percent trust in pesticides and to reach for the Killmaster when problems with bugs arose. (Actually, chlorpyrifos was the most widely used household pesticide in America until the EPA required the Dow Chemical Corporation to severely limit its use on crops and prohibited its use where children could be exposed. Dow, however, *yet* markets the stuff for home use in developing countries.) The knowledge of years past when organic practice didn't even know it was organic practice was not taught to me. I would have to wing it.

The first thing I did was go to the hardware store and buy a strip of yellow plastic covered with really sticky stuff that said it was environmentally friendly and would kill whitefly, fungus gnats, winged aphids, cucumber beetles, fruit flies, leafminers, and leaf hoppers. Heck, I didn't even know what some of those things were, but I could guess I didn't want them in my garden, and if I could send them off in an environmentally friendly way, I would jump at the chance.

I hung a couple of strips in the garden. A few days later I checked them. The trap did indeed capture a slew of whiteflies and a raft of gnats. However, it also caught two ladybird beetles. Not only did I feel bad about the ladybirds (it was bad enough that their houses were continually on fire while their children were home), but just one ladybird beetle will eat a hundred aphids a day, maybe five thousand in the course of its lifetime, and a ladybug larva will eat one hundred aphids *an hour.* In one fell sticky swoop I had put myself deeply in the hole on the pest-accounting sheet.

The supposed earth-friendly sticky traps were obviously not the way to go. And the Quarter-Acre Farm was quickly being bitten and chewed and swallowed by insects. The fruit trees were thick with scale, the vegetables were flocked by aphids. There were ornate patterns eaten through the cabbage and the artichoke leaves. I was edging closer to breaking out the chemicals when I saw a lazy flight of beetles around a young cherry tree. The tree's branches were flocked with scale insects.

Upon closer inspection, and a quick trip to my *Guide to North American Insects,* I ascertained the bugs were assassin beetles, which sounded promising. I expected the things to dispatch scale with the finesse of a six-legged Jackie Chan. Instead, they landed with the grace of an albatross then bumbled around the branches of the cherry tree like dozens of Mr. Magoos. I watched one small assassin stumble up and down a twig, repeatedly missing a clump of scale by half a centimeter. I finally gave up my vigil in disgust, thinking the naming of the bug was some gardener's bitter joke.

The next day, however, the small tree had been virtually cleared of scale. It turns out that while an Assassin bug does indeed fly slowly and seem absurdly clumsy, it has lightning fast front legs, which they use to snatch their victims (with such a struggle to stumble into its prey, I'd hope they'd at least be brilliant at catching it once they did). They then inject their prey with paralyzing venom and use a straw-like mouth characteristic of true bugs, called a stylet, to devour their meal.

If assassin beetles could clear my tree of scale with such ease, could I get them to take care of the aphids too? What other insect carnivores could take care of my gardening woes? I need only find the right appetite to match my garden's destructive insect entrees. It wasn't a new idea. In ancient China, predaceous ants were used to protect citrus crops. Though I didn't think I had any ants in my garden that were able to do much of anything helpful, I knew that there were other bugs that could. The first step was to identify the insects that were doing damage. Problem pests included scale, aphids, tomato hornworms, cabbage moths, mosquitoes, and whitefly.

Next, I looked up what ate these creatures and made a wish list for the beneficials I needed. I figured if I could host assassin bugs (soldiers), ladybugs, lacewings, dragonflies, and praying mantises in my garden, I would be in good shape.

But then came the hard part. How could I get these hungry insects into my garden and keep them there? I was told that ladybugs released into your garden most often flew right out of it again. Further, it is the ladybug larvae (spiky alligator-like creatures) that are the true insect-eating machines. Praying mantises and lacewing eggs had to be sent through the mail, which seemed a bit iffy, and it didn't seem possible at all to import dragonflies. It seemed if I really wanted insect helpers in my garden, I would have to *invite* them, and futher, make my garden a place they wanted to remain.

The most compelling invitation is flowers. It seemed strange to be planting flowers to attract carnivorous insects, but a mere smorgasbord of scale, aphids, and cabbage worms is not going to get your insect pals to leave their metaphorical toothbrushes in your medicine cabinet. They don't know about the insect smorgasbord in the first place because the smorgasbord doesn't want to get eaten, so it hides.

Flowers signal to a carnivorous insect that there is a place it is likely to get a meal because their *prey* is attracted to flowers. In addition, many carnivorous insects also eat nectar, and even fruit or pollen, in addition to meat. Though flowers might seem an obvious sign of nectar availability, many plants have "extrafloral nectaries"—often a modified plant margin, plant hair, or leaf margin that produces nectar to not only attract beneficial insects but to also keep them around during the lull between spikes in the plant's pest population.

And I couldn't forget that even if an insect was a predator, it was also likely prey to some other bug and therefore needed hiding places if it was going to call my yard home. Further, insects were ever on the lookout for a good nursery for their future progeny. Flowers, shrubs, and even mulch provide cover for eggs and larvae as well as the adult insects.

Some of the plants that are best for wooing insects are angelica, bee balm, buckwheat, calendula, carrot (let a few bolt and flower), ceanothus, cilantro, clover, daisy, loveage, parsley, queen ann's lace, snowberry sunflower, alyssum, thyme, and yarrow. These are but a few possibilities.

Water is part of the invitation as well. While some carnivorous insects get most of their moisture from the blood of their victims (bwa ha ha ha) many drink from dew, puddles, and the edge of ponds. If the weather is particularly dry you could put some water in a saucer of pebbles for your insect guests. At the Quarter-Acre Farm, we have a fishpond and water buckets for the chickens and geese that insects can also partake of.

A year after making a concerted effort to make our yard an attractive environment to beneficials, I would say natural predators take care of most of the insect problems on the Quarter-Acre Farm. Most—but not all. Ants, for example, were protecting some of the scale and aphids from the predatory insects. Ants and aphids enjoy an intriguing relationship called mutualism. A "you scratch my back and I'll scratch yours" kind of thing. But rather than scratching, there's a lot of sucking, excreting, and petting going on instead. Aphids are doing the sucking, siphoning the sap of phloem vessels in plants with specialized mouthparts called stylets from their plant of choice. These fluids are rather weak in the nitrogen department, however, and the insects have to suck down a lot of it to get enough nutritive value. All of that sap and there's going to be a lot of waste product as well. This waste product is called honeydew and it practically *rains* from the recta of the aphids.

You might be saying Ewww! right now, but ants are saying, Mmmmm! Ants love honeydew so much that they will risk their lives to protect the aphids from predators and parasites in order to maintain a steady stream of this recta manna.

Once I saw this sordid partnership going on, I spread a rather icky petroleum jelly-meets-super glue substance called Tanglefoot around the circumference of the base of the tree, creating a barrier that ants could not cross.

The unguarded aphids were soon dispatched by ladybugs. Sometimes the volume of scale or aphids seemed just too much to believe that even an army of ladybugs could take care of the problem. Aphids can reproduce without having sex in a process called parthenogenesis. A newly born aphid becomes a reproducing adult within a week. It then produces up to five offspring per day for up to fifty days.

The eighteenth-century French naturalist René Antoine Ferchault de Reaumur estimated that if all the descendants from a single aphid survived and were arranged in a line four abreast, that line would exceed the length of the circumference of the globe. I believe it because most of them were on my broccoli.

When the beneficials seemed to need a little help, I sprayed the aphid-riddled plants with a blast of water to knock the bugs off. Apparently aphids are pretty weak; even those that fly don't fly much and most can't even do that. Climbing back up the stems for them would be like me taking on Kilimanjaro. The unmoored insects quickly die.

Though spraying plants is helpful in some ways, in others it can be costly. Ladybugs lay their eggs on protected leaves and stems close to their prey, and while you're jetting off a few hundred aphids, you might also be destroying a few hundred future ladybug larvae who would have wolfed the fallen aphids down in an hour and moved on to eat another bucketful. I try to check for the yellow to orange spindle-shaped eggs before I turn on the force.

The cabbageworms were another problem that took longer to solve than I would have liked. They are the exact color of broccoli and have a grip like limpets. The combination of these characteristics pretty much ensured that I would be steaming them up with the broccoli and serving them to my grossed-out family. (What's worse than finding a boiled caterpillar on your pasta? Finding half of one.) They also, as their name would imply, were chomping the heck out of the cabbage.

I found a folk remedy online that said I could protect my cruciferous vegetables by sprinkling them with cornmeal. The caterpillars would eat the cornmeal, which—to put it delicately—they are unable to expel, and would die of the ensuing blockage. Not only did that seem a horrific way to kill something (what's worse than finding half a cabbageworm on your pasta? Finding an exploded one), for several reasons, it didn't make sense.

Didn't cabbageworms prefer cabbage to cornmeal? So wouldn't they just eat around it? And if they could digest cabbage, why would they have such problems with corn?

My entomologist friend, Diane, said that she'd never heard of caterpillar murder by corn stoppage, but if I wanted to get rid of cabbageworms, I should use the bacterium *Bacillus thuringiensis* (Bt). It sounded like something Monsanto would have come up with, but Diane said it was a naturally occurring biologic agent found in soil worldwide and its insecticidal activity was discovered about a hundred years ago. After the bacterium infects the insect larvae, she explained, the bacteria begin to produce an endotoxin. The infection spreads and the endotoxins rise, which quickly proves fatal to the caterpillar. Not only does Bt do-in the dastardly brassica eaters, but it is extremely narrow in its effects, only putting caterpillars out of transmission. If a bird, a ladybug, a dog, or Louis happened to accidentally eat, say, *half* of a treated worm, there would be no ill effects whatsoever.

I hurried off to the garden center and bought a bottle, then hurried home and sprayed my cabbage plants. Soon I was caterpillar free. The bacillus worked like a charm. And I'm not the only one to have noticed its charm-working skills. Companies have now engineered plants that express the endotoxin directly without the help of the bacteria. Unfortunately, insects are now quickly building resistance to the plant-expressed endotoxin, something that didn't happen quickly with the natural bacterium. Turns out, the endotoxin worked in concert with an entire infection process initiated by the bacterium, one that is difficult for insects to protect against, and one that ultimately kills. Oops.

Sometimes it seems that science is the environment's brilliant little sister, watching, learning, growing, and is mostly incredibly cool and much loved. Yet, though brilliant, she's also sometimes a sophomoric, bratty, and irresponsible little sister, so that Environment keeps shouting to Mother Nature, "Mo-*ther!* Tell Science to keep out of my stuff! She keeps messing everything up!" In fact, I often feel that Environment is screaming that until I can grow up, to keep out of her stuff as well.

And so it is not surprising to me, as I ponder my waxing and waning garden skills, that all the insect-wrangling methods I found that worked in my garden—planting insect-friendly plants, utilizing barrier methods, spraying insects with water, hand picking pests from the plants, and employing the biologic agency of bacillus—are not chemically (or otherwise) one-upping nature, but utilizing the already set functions of flora and fauna (of which I try to consider myself a part).

What *is* surprising is that most of those methods likely hearken from the time man and bug first went head to head over the same piece of fruit in the garden. It makes me laugh (bitterly, oh so bitterly) that, except for hand picking the bugs from my crops, which reflects a pretty basic "Ack! There's a *bug* on my bean!" reaction, which might well be genetic, I learned about these things with the same astonishment I would have felt had Steven Hawking just invented them.

It reminds me of the old joke, "When I was fourteen my parents were so ignorant I could hardly stand them, but when I got to be twenty-one, I was astonished by how much they had learned in seven years."

Some of us take a bit longer than others.

Figs and Goat Cheese

What better way to enjoy figs (pollinated by wasps) than with goat cheese, honey (made by bees), wrapped in prosciutto, and broiled . . .

Ingredients:

▶ As many figs as you'd like

For each fig:

▶ 1 TB goat cheese

▶ drizzle of honey

▶ a thin slice of prosciutto

1. Wash the figs.

2. Score an X in the top of each fig and take a sphere of goat cheese (one

of those little melon ballers works perfectly for this) and tamp it into the scored fig.

3. If you like, dress your fig in a cape of transparently thin prosciutto. If not, leave the plump girls unabashedly naked.

4. Put your stuffed, dressed figs, now looking like dowagers going to the opera, on a cookie sheet and warm them up under the broiler.

5. When the cheese is soft and the cape is crisping along the edges, take the figs out and soothe them with a drizzle of wildflower honey. Serve warm.

POLE DANCING

*"The pumpkins were growing so fast
they dragged themselves to death."*
—SPIKE HAIGLER

By the time I had the weeds and bugs sorted out, weather was turning, and thoughts were turning as well—to the holidays. Halloween and Thanksgiving were coming up and pumpkins were everywhere. *Giant* pumpkins.

Christy Harp, an Ohio math teacher, grew the 2009 world record pumpkin weighing in at 1,725 pounds. At our house, we began guessing at the math problems Christy might formulate for her students. "If a pumpkin grew in girth eastward from Findley at a speed of 200 mph and another grew westward from Canton at a third of that speed, which pumpkin would arrive in Mansfield first?"

I couldn't find any proof that Christy had made up gourd-specific math problems, but she did say that at the height of her prize-winning pumpkin's growing period it was putting on thirty-three pounds *a day*. I was amazed; not even during the chocolate season between Halloween and Easter have I managed that. I was also amazed at the sheer size of the "finished" pumpkin and began to fantasize over the pumpkin pies,

the pumpkin ravioli, and the soups that such a pumpkin could make. I do love pumpkin. Unfortunately, the trouble I faced with growing pumpkins on the Quarter-Acre Farm was the room a pumpkin—indeed *all* of the winter squashes—needed in order to grow that put them on the bottom of the vegetable efficiency chart.

Why do the winter squashes, which include delicious types such as spaghetti squash, butternut, acorn, pink banana, kabocha, and of course pumpkin, require so much space?

Since *most* pumpkins do not attain the girth of elephant seals, the size of the produce itself is not the problem. The actual rub is that pumpkins grow their fruit along vines, and the vines can get as much as thirty feet long. The vines love to ramble and their leaves tend to be huge.

Certainly, the times I had attempted to grow squashes I ended up with an area of my yard that we referred to as the "squash jungle" because it quickly became so overgrown it was impenetrable. Squash grew and died there before I even knew they'd flowered. I would often discover the fruit lying on the ground like disfigured limbs after mildew or frost had killed off the leaves.

Worse, the rampaging plants would usually overrun the less mobile vegetables I had planted. Watching the garden become overtaken by a full-depth green avalanche made me think of my great-great-Uncle Spike's tall-tale letter to my father when he was a boy reporting that the pumpkins were growing so fast they'd dragged themselves to death.

I thought maybe I would skip growing pumpkins on the Quarter-

Acre Farm and stick to the better-behaved vegetables, like beans. Then again, beans grew on vines, long messy ones, as well. They didn't have as large of leaves, but still . . . it got me thinking. Why not grow squash on a trellis or a pole?

I pounded some eight-foot tree stakes into the dirt, screwed some deck screws into the stakes for the vines to hold on to, and planted several pumpkin seeds at their base. I also planted some seeds on a length of chicken wire stretched across an old swing set we had never managed to remove from the backyard (crafted and set in concrete circa 1950 when they apparently made swing sets to last through an atomic blast for the children to play on when they emerged from the shelter). The little plants poked their tender heads through the soil a week later, and soon after that the first problem presented itself.

It wasn't one vine that grew from each plant, but two. Then from the two vines grew even more vines. No wonder a jungle grew from the ovoid seeds. I managed to drape the many vines along the chicken wire, but it was way too bushy to manage on the pole.

So I pruned. I twined the primary and secondary vines around the pole, but I promptly snipped any vine that grew off of those. It didn't seem to harm the plant at all. Problem solved!

But as weeks passed, I saw that none of the plants on the trellis or on the pole seemed as vigorous as the plants I had allowed to meander on the ground in the past. The problem was, pumpkins are what are referred to as "heavy feeders." Imagine the football player in high school who answers the incredulous question, "How can you eat so much?" with, "I'm a big boy, I need big food."

Pumpkins are the linebackers of the vegetable world. They need lots of food to nourish them, and since they are also about 80 percent water, they also need to take in volumes of that as well. Because of this, pumpkins grow roots *along* their vines, rather than just beneath the base of the plant, to take in extra food and water. By growing my plants in the air, I was depriving them of the means to supply themselves with extra nutrition. I was starving my pumpkins.

This could not stand. If I had put my squash on a diet worthy of an upcoming 20th high school reunion, I could yet turn it around and provide a pumpkin smorgasbord to chub those big boys up. I stepped up the water and ground-dressed the soil around the pumpkins with extra compost and rabbit manure, scratching it in carefully so as to not disturb the roots. I repeated the top dressing every couple of weeks and also provided a "vegetable big gulp" every week—this one made of compost tea. I kept up their special linebacker feeding and watering regimen as they produced their fruit.

Problem solved. The vines perked up and looked much healthier. Certain I was on my way now and hoping to maintain my forward momentum, I even worked to ensure pollination. I cut the male flowers (which have a pollen-covered pad called an anther on top of a small, ahem, shaft inside the flower), peeled back the petals, and rubbed them on the female flowers (which have a sticky roundish thing called a stigma inside the flower and an ovary which looks like, and actually is, a tiny fruit behind the flower). Feeling a little dirty and kinky on top of it, I was rewarded for my deviant behavior with nascent pumpkins that soon swelled to the size of ping pong balls, then tennis balls, and soon began approaching volleyball size. At this rate, we would have so many pumpkins we could store some to eat and Jesse would be able to replicate his California snowman display—pumpkins stacked like balls of snow, replete with stick arms and carrots for the nose.

It all fell apart after that, literally. The trellis collapsed—*and* I lost a pumpkin from the poles because the stem snapped.

Part of the problem was a weenie trellis, but another reason for the collapse was that no matter all its tendrils, pumpkins are creepers and they don't hold on very well. Further, a gallon of water weighs about eight pounds, so a volleyball-sized pumpkin is no featherweight. I could see why my weeny *trellis* collapsed with the unbalanced weight of four or five pumpkins on it, but what amazed me was that an inch-thick woody pumpkin *stem* wasn't tough enough to take what I figured was a mere five pounds at most.

Unfortunately, pumpkin stems (or *peduncles* if you prefer a more scientific and highly amusing term) are notoriously brittle. You can go online and read accounts of the many ways in which people like Christy Harp protect their giant pumpkin's stems, practically from the time of pollination, against any sort of pressures that might result in the dreaded *stem stress*: positioning the plant to the perfect angle, and never, *ever* moving the pumpkin, of *any* size, unless it is done in tiny increments over many days.

I solved these new problems by first reinforcing the chicken wire. I also made each pumpkin its own hammock. I knew that pumpkins were prone to rot if they sat on a wet surface, so the pumpkins had to have hammocks with circulation. Oranges also need circulation; that's why they are sold in those net bags—net bags, I might add, that I had been saving for ages *having known,* as I'd told Louis, *I would have a use for them someday.* The net bags did make ideal supports for the pumpkins. (The bags also made ideal supports for muskmelons and watermelons as well, as I applied the pumpkin-on-a-pole system to other plants. The bags will also leave a lovely lacy pale yellow pattern where it keeps the sun from the watermelons' green skin.)

When my pumpkins turned bright orange, I cut the tough, if brittle, peduncles and placed the pumpkins on a bed of straw in the cool garage. One might think pumpkins are dead at this point, but they are still living entities; one of the reasons they keep so long.

To keep the living pumpkins in storage, one must treat them almost as well as when they were on the vine. Luckily you don't have to water and feed them, but you must prepare them for what I think of as "pumpkin hibernation." A stored pumpkin should have about four inches of stem intact, and a cured skin (from sitting off the vine post-harvest in 80 degrees with good air circulation for a few days) to slow respiration rates. The skin should have no injuries that would allow rot-producing organisms to enter. The pumpkins should be stored on a porous surface in a cool room protected from extreme heat and cold. In this way, pumpkins and other winter squash will last for months. You will be assured of having pumpkins all winter for pumpkin pie, pumpkin soup, California snowmen, and best of all, pasta con zucca.

Pasta con Zucca

I began making ravioli con zucca, or squash ravioli, for a friend who took students to Italy each year. He would make a pilgrimage to a particular city in order to go to a particular restaurant just to eat a particular dish of Ravioli con zucca. I haven't had the privilege of eating that particular Italian establishment's ravioli, but mine, if I do say so myself, are particularly delicious. They're also *time-consuming* since I make them with homemade pasta, inside of which I put a mixture of pumpkin, amaretti cookies, and Parmesan cheese.

This recipe is my *un*constructed version of the meal, and while it is just as good (perhaps better because you can bump up the squash-to-pasta ratio by merely preparing an additional squash or a bigger one for the meal), it is also a hundred (a thousand!) times easier, *much less* time-consuming, and virtually un-screw-up-able.

You may use almost any orange-fleshed sweet winter squash (pumpkin, kabocha, Hubbard) for this dish. In fact, even sweet potatoes would be delicious.

Ingredients:

- 4 to 6 cups cubed squash (of your choice)
- 1 to 2 cups sage leaves
- 8 oz. linguine
- 1 cup shredded parmesan cheese
- 1 stick butter
- 2 TB dark-brown sugar
- olive oil

1. Place the ½ inch cubes of squash into a bowl.

2. Drizzle the squash with olive oil and sprinkle the dark brown sugar over the top.

3. Stir until the moisture from the squash, the olive oil, and the brown sugar combines to form a thick juice to envelope each squash cube.

4. Pour the squash onto a lipped cookie sheet, spreading the squash into a single layer.

5. Place squash in oven and roast at 450. When the squash has browned, there will be a slightly caramelized skin around each cube and the center of each will be tender.

6. As the squash roasts, melt a cube of butter in a saucepan, adding in a large handful of de-stemmed sage leaves (the more the better if you ask me—even two cups!). Allow the butter to barely, *barely* bubble. Within about 15 minutes, the sage leaves will be crispy. (Truly, this is delicious.)

7. As the butter bubbles, and the roasted squash cools slightly, cook the linguine in salted water.

8. When the linguine is cooked and drained, place in a large bowl and toss with the butter and sage and a big handful of shredded Parmesan.

9. Place the squash over the top of the linguine (to avoid having the squash gravitate to the bottom of the bowl, do not toss with the butter and parmesan) and serve with a green salad. Mangia!

WATER

"Uncle Sam took up the challenge in the year of '33
For the farmer and the factory and all of you and me.
He said 'Roll along Columbia. You can ramble out to sea.
But river while you're ramblin' you can do some work for me.'"
—WOODY GUTHRIE

CHAPTER
FOURTEEN

My father was a civil engineer; water systems were his business. Considering the many years he spent designing water treatment centers, I should have picked up some knowledge of fluid dynamics and volume computations. Somehow I missed my chance. The one thing I *did* manage to remember about his job is a pen he brought home on which was printed *It may be sewage to you, but it's my bread and butter.*

There is something sort of magical about turning on a spigot to conjure water. It was a feeling reinforced when we moved into our house, which had an automatic water system to keep the two swaths of lawn, front and back, nice and green. The sprinklers seemed mysteriously called to rise and rain, beckoned in the summer dawn by what could have been the crook of a water nymph's finger, as *I* reclined happily in bed.

When we got rid of the lawn, however, the nymph-powered water system was no longer useful, throwing its morning deluge willy-nilly into places that didn't need irrigation. Therefore, in order to keep the vegetables watered and not waste water in between the beds, I watered by hand.

At its best, watering by hand gave me a chance to know my plants and contemplate the reasons why they were succumbing to disease, drying up, or being eaten by something. But as I put in more and more beds and planted more and more seeds, I found that hand watering took too long, and I wasn't doing such a hot job of it to boot. I was going to have to learn something about water systems after all.

One of my first ideas was to pour water down a series of half-sawn PVC pipes that I had strategically drilled holes into where the plants needed water; a sort of Roman aqueduct idea.

I had always envisioned the Roman aqueducts as something like a waterslide at Wet and Wild, water racing downhill at a 90 degree grade and splashing down in fountains all around the ancient cities. Instead the reality is even more impressive. The Pont du Gard aqueduct, which transported five million gallons of water *a day* to Rome, was fifty miles long. And instead of dropping precipitously, the aqueducts had the amazing gradient of only about eleven inches of drop for each half mile of length. Over a fifty mile length, there is only about eighteen yards of height difference between the beginning of the water's journey and its end. The idea is staggering.

Sadly, I am no Roman (or any other kind of) engineer. My PVC aqueducts didn't work. Water poured over the ends, didn't drip out the too-small holes, or poured too quickly out the too-large holes; all sizes of holes clogged, and plants expired due to dehydration or drowning.

Water is incredibly difficult to control since it is amazingly sensitive to speed and drop and gravity. While the Romans used this to great advantage, I was obviously a water idiot. I turned hopefully to a more modern method of transporting water: weeping hoses made from recycled bicycle tires. This worked pretty well. Because I was constantly moving my raised beds, the weeping hoses allowed me to reconfigure the watering "system" to fit the beds. I put snap-on ends on the hoses so that when I wanted to water, I pulled the regular hose over, snapped it on the weeping hose, and turned it on for an hour or so.

One problem with this system was the fact that the hose watered between the beds as well; I tried to remedy the situation by placing pots of onions under those areas (and so tripped over them all season). My other problem was that I would forget to turn the hoses off.

I had a partial success when I created my "octo-hose" system. Louis, Sam, and I were going out of town for two weeks, and I needed to simplify my shifting watering system so our garden-sitter could water. I bought some triple brass manifolds and hooked up eight garden hoses to splits so that all of the weeping hoses could run at once. Eight hoses could be turned on and the entire garden could be watered in a couple of hours a couple of times a week. Of course, with turquoise and forest green hose tendrils snaking across pathways and up beds, the garden looked like a Rube Goldberg production or something out of a science fiction movie. Not very attractive, but it worked. We returned from vacation and the garden looked greener than it ever had. And our neighbor who had watched the garden was not only still on speaking terms with us but also said the watering had been *easy*. Of course he was also watching the geese, so in comparison I suspect almost anything would seem easy. I continued to happily use the octo-hose system for weeks—until we got our water bill.

It was huge.

Partially, this was because I absent-mindedly left the hoses on, and also, though I tried to save the water wasted between beds, I knew I wasn't doing a very good job of it. Further, I suspected that even as I was keeping some of my poor plants in a state of thirstiness, I was over watering many others.

I started fantasizing about introducing an urban farming bill to the state legislature that would subsidize the water bills of residents who grew vegetables in more than 50 percent of their yard, but until I got that passed, I decided I'd better think about the quality of my watering.

The first step to being a better resource manager was to admit that I watered visually. If the soil around the plants *looked* dry, I watered until it looked good and wet. If the plants *looked* wilted, I watered. The trouble with watering visually is that, unless you have X-ray vision, you can't see what's going on where it matters—that is, underground and in the plants' own living systems.

I soon realized I needed to know what kind of underground I had. If I had sandy loam, water was going to move through and across it in a different way than if I had clay. Water moves through a sandy soil quickly and narrowly, taking a mere 24 hours to percolate six feet down (due to gravity), and its horizontal reach (through capillary action) will only be about ten to twelve inches. Water through clay soil won't reach six feet for 48 hours, but in that time the water will extend a full thirty inches horizontally. Clay stores water for a much longer time as well.

I had clay soil, but there was more to being an educated waterer than just knowing that. In his book *Grow More Vegetables,* John Jeavons pointed out that when we water, we are not really watering plants. What we are doing is watering the soil so that the *soil* can water the plants. Therefore, to know how well your soil is watering your plants, one must keep in mind things like "penetration factors." Penetration factors include the dampness of soil and the size of soil "pores," which are the spaces between the aggregates that make up the dirt.

Damp soil will conduct water to your plant's roots better and farther than dry soil will. Try taking a dry sponge and mopping up a spill, then try using a damp sponge. The damp sponge will take in the spill much easier. Damp dirt will take in a spill of water the same way.

If you have a good variety of sizes of soil pieces (and therefore a well balanced porosity), water (and air) will also move well and a crust will not form on the surface (one of the problems of my disastrous soil purchase).

Why this makes such a difference to a plant is due to a plant's system. Plants want three underground things all at once. They want water, nutrients, and air. If one waters too much, not only is there not enough air for the plant's roots, but nutrients can also be leached away. If there is not enough water, the plants will wilt, and a hormonal imbalance within the plant will occur, causing poor bud formation and fruit drop—in other words, it will fail to thrive. Further, if the plant does not feel good, water-wise, then the stomata of the plant's leaves will not open to conserve its water. If the stomata do not open, then CO_2 cannot go in, and photosynthesis will not occur.

As a person whose brain is akin to a colander, this was a lot for me to remember. Further, while I knew different plants had different water needs, I also seemed to recollect that the different water-needing plants needed that water *differently* at different times of their growing cycles! Some plants, like grapes, even respond better to having their water restricted entirely for a span of time.

It was too much for me to keep straight. I imagined giving up farming altogether. Instead I decided I would try to remember a few simple things, and the nuances would come to me later.

1. The shorter the root, the more often a plant needs to be watered since water is lost from the top of the bed first. Seeds have the shortest roots of all, of course, and so no matter what kind of plant they are, they need constant dampness (but not necessarily deep dampness). Lettuce—short roots. Carrots, beets, radishes—also short roots.

2. The longer the root, the deeper the watering, but with less frequency. Tomatoes have really long roots. That's why my friend Al's suffer-and-save advice was so good.

3. When plants are making their edible parts, they need more water than when they are just making leaves.

4. Put like-rooted vegetables together.

I also bought a moisture meter so that I could get a feel for how long my dirt was staying damp—underground, where it mattered.

Now how to make it happen. I continued to use the weeping drip hoses on the lines of fruit trees. They were close enough together that no water was wasted between them, and they all had roughly the same water needs. But for the raised beds, I was once again going to try a drip system.

I had tried a drip system years ago. I hated it. The tubing wouldn't lie flat, I punched holes in the wrong places, put the elbows an inch too far one direction or another and I couldn't fix it because the compression fittings could not be removed and reset. Not only that, my drippers clogged and when I changed my garden around, and I couldn't reconfigure the system.

But that was a long time ago, and technology marches on. I now planned to use a permalock system. Contrary to what it sounds like, the components were reusable. I would also use cleanable drippers and make the holes with a pliers-like tool rather than struggling with a tool that looked like an ice pick.

Also, I made a point of watching how-to videos. For a visual learner like me, seeing someone actually putting a system together was invaluable. Plus, they provided lots of hints and suggestions.

First, I took a map of my garden and configured my watering plan. Then I made a list of what I needed to make it happen. This is when I realized that I *had* actually learned some water-related things from my dad. I knew how to "plumb" and knew what tees, elbows, female pipe ends, male pipe ends, and the like were. I expertly(ish) figured the number of elbows and tees I would need.

After the supplies came in, Jesse came over to take a look. This was a parental dream. His decade-long practice with Legos (and my decade-long practice of stepping, barefooted, on them) had come to some good. Who knew that building flying cars, bridges, and Hot Wheel garages with little plastic blocks was eventually going to translate into something useful? He eyed the landscape, made some changes in my watering plan, and got to work.

Jesse and I unrolled yards and yards of quarter-inch, black plastic piping. (It uncoils best if you've got a warm day in which to work so the plastic softens.) Jesse cut and placed sections with the aplomb of . . . yes, a kid putting a toy together. The process was akin to setting up a miniature highway system full of interchanges and off-ramps and even highway closures.

The main pipes ran the length of the garden, and elbows and tees sent minor roads to the individual beds. Off those roads came tiny little county roads, which ended at the bases of plants with little sprinklers and drippers. Jesse made those little flexible pipes very long so that they could be moved from plant to plant as needed for subsequent plantings. Jesse also put off/on valves at the junction of some beds, such as the melon beds, so that I could water them more often than other beds, such as the tomatoes.

Once we got the system working, Jesse shallowly buried most of the "highway" system, leaving only the black pipe visible at the beds themselves. It seemed perfect.

Then I found the grapes weren't being watered, and neither was one of my side beds . . . and the potatoes were getting too much water and one of the spigots wasn't spraying. The back seemed to have great water pressure but not the front, and speaking of the front, we hadn't put a valve on the system to turn it off when I wanted to use the hose.

I hated to tell Jesse, but he took it in stride. "You'll find all sorts of ways you need it to change," he said. Then he showed me how to do it myself. How things change.

I'm not as good at configuring and putting together the water system as Jesse yet, but he did have those years of Lego building, which I failed to benefit from. Still, I'm doing okay—the drip system is working so much better than my octo-hose system, and it's costing us less in the water department; it is most gratifying, and I believe it will keep getting better.

In the meantime, however, I'm drawing up my proposal for urban-farming water breaks.

Iced Tea with Lavender, Lemon Verbena, and Mint

When it is hot and your plants are crying out for water, it's likely that you're doing the same. And while water is about the best thing going (for some reason, when I was a kid it tasted best out of the hose), iced tea is a close second.

We make sun tea in a flat glass refrigerator pitcher that has a stopper and a wide opening. The wide opening is a must or it will be nigh impossible to clean the pitcher, and you will be fishing out tea bags and herbs with a wire coat hanger.

Ingredients:

▶ 1 gallon water

▶ 4 tea bags such as PG Tips' Red Rose

▶ 2 TB lavender flowers

▶ 1 cup mint

After the sun tea has brewed, you have two options for flavoring it with herbs. You can add the herbs to the pitcher itself, or you can add them to the glasses. It's all about presentation at this point. I can see putting sprigs of herbs in cups on the table for a summer soiree and letting guests choose their own particular favorites to muddle into chilled glasses with their tea. Usually, however, I put the herbs straight into my half gallon refrigerator pitcher, using the nonbusiness end of a wooden spoon to muddle (or mush/crush/mistreat) the herbs to release their flavors, so I can grab a glass of the refreshing concoction fast. It's very la-di-dah.

WHAT WEIGHS MORE, A POUND OF DIAMONDS OR A POUND OF MUSHROOMS?

"Shitake happens"
—SEEN ON A T-SHIRT

Let me apologize for this year's Christmas present. It may be the worst homemade gift yet in the long line of horrible homemade gifts that I have been responsible for. Worse than the hand-dipped candles that had beads of water trapped between the layers of wax so that as the candles burned they sporadically hissed as if the candles disapproved of the dinner on the table, or the diners themselves, or life in general—sometimes they hissed so much so that they extinguished themselves altogether in the middle of a meal.

This year's present was also worse than the fish-print aprons that I didn't wash before packaging up and sending out, so that when people opened the gift a week or two later, the smell of rotted halibut slammed out of the box.

This year I gave bags of used coffee grounds that required the recipient to mist them with water every day until the grounds were covered with disgusting furry growths. The recipients of these "gifts" then felt like failures and surreptitiously threw the gifts away thinking they had done something wrong, vowing they must never let on what they'd allowed to happen.

I might as well have shouted, "Happy holidays! You get a tedious, repetitive chore resulting in moldy trash *and* a of sense shame, to top it all!"

Those bags of coffee grounds were inoculated with mushroom spore and were *supposed* to produce lovely, tender mushrooms for all of you to enjoy. *Really.* I promise.

Mushrooms seemed an ideal crop to grow during the winter at the Quarter-Acre Farm. I could grow them in my garage, or even—because our house was built in California during the insulation-challenged 1950s—in my office where it was cool and damp until mid May.

I started my mushroom-growing career by buying a mushroom kit from an online mushroom supply store. When the kit arrived, it looked like something Count Dracula would send ahead in preparation for a visit: a box of dirt. The instructions promised that if I were to gently rake the surface of the dirt, mist it, and keep the whole shebang in a dark place, I would be rewarded with a bumper crop of crimini mushrooms.

During the ensuing days, the box of dirt grew a webby sort of growth and then did indeed bloom, thrillingly, with criminis. I harvested bunches and bunches of them. I sautéed them, grilled them, then made mushroom soup. The mushroom soup was a particular pleasure because it was so easy and *amazingly delicious*. The only other mushroom soup I had ever eaten was Campbell's Cream of Mushroom Soup. As a kid I'd found the pallid glutinous dreck so disgusting I had never managed to overcome my aversion to it and try mushroom soup of any other ilk—until my own homegrown, homemade concoction.

I was so excited by the pleasure of mushrooms and the ease of growing them that I told Jesse I was going to grow portobellos next. Jesse told me that I was *already* growing portobellos—portobellos are merely grown up criminis, usually a whopping three to seven days older. Apparently, they taste a bit different not only because they are older but also because they have opened (their gills exposed to air) and have lost a little moisture, making them meatier (which also makes them an excellent candidate for grilling).

Of course I thought, how could I have forgotten Jesse's mushroom stage? During his time at the University of California, Jesse had taken a class in mycology. I have to admit that made me a little uneasy, especially because every time I mentioned that my son was studying mushrooms in college and loving it, my friends would snort and say, "Of *course* he is."

Then there was the great delaminating.

That year for Sam's birthday, Jesse promised to make Sam, who was doing a lot of cooking at the time, a mushroom farm. Jesse came over on a Thursday evening with a bag of barley, some mushroom spawn, and a request to use our pressure cooker.

I pulled out the pressure cooker and some canning jars, then Louis and I went out (fled, actually) to dinner. Several hours later—luckily after a glass or two of wine—I called the house to check on the boys. Sam answered, and with a certain amount of uncharacteristic glee in his voice, reported an explosion, smoke, and his certainty that the pressure cooker was no longer going to be of any use.

Jesse and Sam assured me that although the smoke alarms had proved in good working order, they were in no danger. I, in turn, assured them that it was practically impossible to do any permanent damage to a heavy-duty pressure cooker. If anything, the appliance might need a new seal but it would be fine.

However, when Louis and I returned home to a house reeking of smoke, we found that the pressure cooker was indeed ruined. I gaped in grim amazement at the warped discs of copper and steel that had delaminated from the bottom of the pot. I didn't want to imagine what hellish temperature the pot (which had apparently steamed itself dry) must have risen to. But though my pot was damaged, my boys were not, and Sam, for his part, seemed to feel the smoke-filled adventure he'd shared with his brother was well worth the sacrifice of his mushroom farm that year.

Now, as I contemplated growing more Quarter-Acre Farm mushrooms without buying the relatively expensive ready-to-grow kit, Jesse assured me that not only could he help, but that he'd also learned his lesson with the pressure cooker. In fact, we actually could get by without using one at all—which was a good thing since I had never replaced it.

I sent away for a bag of oyster-mushroom spawn. When it arrived,

Jesse and I boiled wood chips for an hour, then drained them and tossed them with the mushroom spawn. We put the chips and spawn in Ziploc vegetable bags (the kind with tiny holes for ventilation), rolled some up in layers of cheesecloth, then put them on trays in the garage and kept them moist.

Once again, success! I cheerfully clipped the white, trumpet-shaped fungus, made more soups, put them in frittatas, and added them to flavorful risotto.

I was gratified not only with the taste of the mushrooms, but also with the ease of substituting the mighty mushroom for meat. If you switched four ounces of mushrooms for four ounces of meat (chopped up in meatballs, or as a Portobello burger, for instance) once a week for a year, you would find yourself not only nutritionally richer, but five pounds lighter at the end of that year.

As a nutritional element, mushrooms are excellent sources of protein, fiber, vitamins C and B, calcium, and minerals; they're also one of the leading sources of two potent antioxidants—selenium and ergothioneine.

Ergothioneine is particularly intriguing, credited with everything from cutting inflammation to increasing sperm viability. Mushrooms have four and twelve times as much of this antioxidant as the two next most powerful sources—chicken livers and wheat germ.

Mushrooms are nutritional powerhouses. It seems that no matter what ails you, there is a mushroom that can either prevent or treat it. And wouldn't it be nice if all medical treatments tasted so good? Mushrooms are chock full of a variety of "volatiles" (chemical compounds released in the mouth) that, depending on the type and concentration, give different mushroom varieties taste characteristics such as "sweet and fruity," "almond-like," "leafy," "pine-tree-like," and "orange and fatty."

Not just humans find them delicious. Almost all animals eat mushrooms, from birds and squirrels to bears and, most famously, pigs. Certainly, Jeannette the goose loves mushrooms. We had a damp bale of straw in the goose pen that sprouted a variety of fungi during the rainy months. I would often see Jeannette delicately snipping and eating the tiny 'shrooms. Perhaps she sensed the mushrooms' nutritional riches. Or perhaps she was just enjoying the effect of a psychotropic fungi, which some animals are notorious for eating.

For instance, psychotropic mushrooms are said to be the source of the myth of Santa's flying reindeer. Lapland reindeer apparently love *Amanita muscaria* mushrooms, which are not only hallucinogenic, but they also supposedly stimulate the animal's muscular system. This made the reindeer's small efforts produce surprising results—*enormous reindeer leaps.* These leaps then led to stories of flying reindeer, which were eventually assimilated into the folklore of St. Nicholas.

I hadn't noticed Jeannette making any grandiose leaps. In fact, on the best of days she could barely manage a three-foot flight. But because Christmas was on my mind, and because I had been having such a good time growing my own (culinary) mushrooms, I decided to share the joy with homemade holiday mushroom kits.

I read that coffee grounds were a wonderful medium for mushroom growing, and I knew where to get a lot of those. I sent away for mushroom spawn, collected the grounds, and acquired coffee bags (the kind you put your beans in at the grocery store) for the containers. When the spawn arrived, I put my small mushroom kits together (spawn in coffee and coffee in bags) and in doing so, made a most grievous error.

I figured the coffee grounds were sterile since they had just been put through a high-temp steam treatment (brewing). Wrong. When growing mushrooms, one should never ever *expect* anything to be sterile, because everything *must* be sterile in order to grow mushrooms.

Why? There are myriad bacteria, molds, and mildews floating around in the air just waiting for a nice place to grow, and most are more vigorous than mushroom spores. Trying to grow mushrooms in contaminated substrate is like plopping an orchid in the ground with weeds growing all around. The weeds are going to overwhelm the orchid, no question. Bacteria and molds, which favor the same conditions that mushrooms do, overwhelm the mushrooms in the same way. The mold called *Trichoderma*, or forest-green mold, is particularly problematic.

Trichoderma is the bane of mushroom growers. If growers spy it in a jar of spawn, without even cracking the lid open, they throw the jar into a vat of boiling water for an hour because *Trichoderma* is so "sticky" it will float through the air, lodge in your hair, on surfaces, and tools, hoping to colonize some poor hardworking mushroom's homeland. Which is likely what happened to my project.

Back to those homemade holiday mushroom farms—I'd like recipients to please no longer think of them as mushroom farms; instead, consider them a different sort of educational gift. What you got was actually a primer, if you will, on molds.

If the mold that grew on your gift of used coffee grounds was not forest green and thus *not* the ubiquitous *Trichoderma*, then perhaps it was cinnamon brown mold, or *Chromelium fulva*. This mold can be yellow-gold, golden brown, or, of course, cinnamon colored.

If the particular mold on your holiday primer was a grayish cobwebby mold, that would be a *Dactylium* mildew. (Isn't this fun?)

Did your mold change from white to pink to cherry red before finally settling on a dull orange? That was *Sporendonema purpurascens*, or lipstick mold.

Your mold might also have been a red bread mold, a *Sepedonium* yellow mold or *Doratomyces*, a black whisker mold.

There, you have just learned a little something about mold. And with that I say, "Ho, ho, ho! Merry Christmas!" (And try not to fret about what you will get from me next year.)

Mushroom Soup

If you look at the ingredients on the can of my childhood enemy—cream of mushroom soup—you'd think it would take a greater intellect than mine to make the stuff. While predictably there are mushrooms in that can, there are also a bevy of non-mushroom ingredients: vegetable oils (from cottonseed to partially hydrogenated soybean), cream, cornstarch, modified food starch, dried whey, soy protein concentrate, monosodium glutamate, whey, calcium caseinate, spice extract, yeast extract, and dehydrated garlic. How could a person possibly figure out how to make mushroom soup on his or her own with a line-up like that?

The reality is, mushroom soup could merely consist of sautéed mushrooms pureed with a bit of broth. Really, that alone would be delicious. But to make my mushroom soup even better, I add onion, celery, and fresh sage, all of which are happily growing on the Quarter-Acre

Farm during the mushroom-damp time of year, which in Northern California runs seemingly interminably from December through March.

Ingredients:
- 2 cups fresh, sliced shitake mushrooms
- ¼ onion, diced
- 1 stalk of celery, diced
- 1/8 cup fresh sage (not packed)
- 2 TB olive oil
- 2 TB salted butter

1. In a large skillet, sauté the onion, celery, and sage in 1 TB of the olive oil until the onion is transparent. Remove the aromatics to a separate bowl.

2. Add the remaining olive oil and butter to the skillet. Melt over medium heat.

3. When the butter is melted, add the cleaned and sliced mushrooms in a single layer and let them cook without touching for 3 to 5 minutes, until the edges begin to brown. Give them a stir, arrange again in a single layer, and let them cook undisturbed until browned.

4. Return the aromatics to the mushrooms and stir.

5. Remove from heat and puree with enough vegetable broth or water to get the preferred creamy-soupy consistency. (My monster Vitamix performs this task in moments and there is not a chunk left in it.)

6. Return the pureed soup to a saucepan, salt to taste, and warm to serving temperature. (If you wish, set aside some of the mushrooms to use as garnish or to add texture to the soup, along with home baked croutons.)

This soup is *so* good and creamy without the cream, and carb-y feeling while being pure vegetable. Mushroom soup is no longer an enemy but the kind of friend who helps you through the cold, grey days of winter. You can't ever have too many of those.

HUNTING SMALL GAME

"The hand that dips into the bottom of the pot
will eat the biggest snail."
—WOLE SOYINKA, NIGERIAN PLAYWRIGHT

When Louis' brother heard about the Quarter-Acre Farm experiment, he asked, "What if a steer wanders into your yard—can she eat that?"

Others wondered if I was going to eat our chickens, our duck, the geese, or the rabbits. I explained we couldn't because we'd already broken the number one tenet of raising livestock: Do not name future meals. But that wasn't the only reason I wasn't tempted to do-in the pets for the sake of *l'orange* sauce. I am simply not crazy about meat. Never have been.

When I was a kid and eating T-bone or roast for the fourth time in a week (my father was a beef and potatoes man), I used to tuck one bite of steak after the other into my cheek, then excuse myself to "use the bathroom." And then I'd spit the stuff in the toilet.

While my disinterest in meat made it easy to forgo entrees from meatloaf to pork loin, as I was living off of my yard, I was looking for other ways to get protein into my diet, especially since I was training for (limping toward) the annual half marathon in Davis, and I needed all the help I could get toward rebuilding my tortured muscles—most of which I hadn't even known were there to begin with.

At about that same time, snails were decimating one of my protein sources: peas. We didn't have the problem in the backyard, where Sunny the duck kept the area pretty much snail-free. But in the front yard, snails were living the good life in the cannas, sealed up in their shells amid the long damp leaves during the day like vampires in a high-rise complex for the undead, then emerging into the evening to suck the life out of the Quarter-Acre flora.

Sam and I did not give up without a fight. We collected the mollusks and then tossed them to Sunny, who waddled at high duck speed toward the tell-tale plop of a snail's landing. Sunny swallowed the snails whole if she couldn't break the shells with her beak. This was alarming because the snails bulged in her feathered neck like pop-it beads, even as she energetically ratcheted her head trying to work the snails to her belly. Sam and I worried we might need to provide serial episodes of the Heimlich maneuver.

Watching Sunny pork-out on her duck escargot, I wondered if there was a difference between *these* garden snails and the snails that humans paid top dollar for at fancy restaurants.

As it turned out, there was nary a one. Our snails were the very same *Helix aspersa*, or petit gris snail, that is served as escargot throughout Europe and the United States. So how did they get here?

Most stories say that *Helix aspersa* was brought to the states by "the French," as though each French citizen arriving in the country tumbled ashore with a pocketful of snails. Other stories narrow it down to the ominous singular: "a Frenchman." There is, however, one story that actually seems to have some backbone to it. In an article titled "Exotic Mollusca in California," which appeared in the April 27, 1900, issue of the journal *Science,* author Robert E. C. Stearns wrote that *Helix aspersa* was "intentionally planted" in California in the 1850's by a Mr. A. Delmas of San Jose. The introduction was "made for edible purposes, or in common parlance, 'with an eye to the pot.' Mrs. Bush of San Jose informs (Mr. Stearns) that the snails have thriven . . . and have multiplied to such an extent, that, in some instances, they are troublesome in the gardens."

Thriven, indeed. Today it is nearly impossible to garden without having to do battle with the pests. Of course, if Mr. Delmas had been successful in turning the tastes of Californians to the flavor of snails (I imagine that skewering them on sticks and deep frying them at the state fair might have been one solution), we wouldn't have such a problem now. Unfortunately, San Franciscans, when presented with the slimy mollusks, pretty much said, "Ewwww, I'm *not* eating that." Which is exactly what Louis said when I told him we could eat our garden snails. Then he added, "You can't be thinking of eating them either. It's crazy; you'll get sick."

Crazy? Snails have been on the human menu since prehistoric days, and ancient Romans prized the things, making "cochlear gardens" in which to fatten them (and season them as well in a stunning example of early modern multi-tasking) on meal, wine, and herbs. In 1885, in his impassioned plea "Why Not Eat Insects?" British writer Vincent Holst called snails, slugs, and insects "clean meat" because their diet consists of wholesome garden greens rather than unpalatable combinations of muck and slop that pigs and fish thrive on. Further, he was perplexed about why we didn't all see snails as a means to end hunger. "Anathematized by every person who possesses the smallest patch of garden, lying in abundance around our feet, a wholesome food, and at the same time a pest to be destroyed, they are still almost entirely neglected by rich and poor alike, though the rich long for new dishes to tempt their faded palates, and the poor starve." A great idea I must say, and if he hadn't gone on to speak in the voice of moths that fly into the candle flame, "Does not the sweet scent of our cooked bodies tempt you? Fry us with butter; we are delicious. Boil us, grill us, stew us; we are good in all ways!" I would have considered him reasonable, indeed.

However, even though I didn't share the bit about moths with Louis, he remained unimpressed. I began soliciting other opinions and found that there was no middle ground to the question of eating snails from the garden. Lots of people were as horrified as Louis, but there were many who said, "Oh sure I'd eat them; I love escargot." Two of my friends were such avid helix-philes (helix-o-philes are collectors of corkscrews) they asked which day they should come by to sample my garden livestock.

To tell the truth, I hadn't actually made up my mind to eat the garden snails. I merely hoped to win the argument over whether or not the snails were edible. But now it seemed I was going to have to put my mollusks where my mouth was.

It would be a party, I decided, with a *lot* of wine served beforehand. Those who refused to eat snails (including my pal Lisa who, in a version of the not-naming-meat rule, said that putting the snails into a terrarium and feeding them made them pets and she couldn't eat pets) would get cheese-stuffed mushroom caps instead.

The first step, one that was by far the easiest, was capturing the snails. I plucked them out of the cannas and from under logs, pulled them like suction cups off step-stones, and when I found them fisted into groups of ten or fifteen in the spaces between dirt and the edges of the raised beds, I collected them like I'd hit, well, pay dirt.

I put my future meal into the *escargotierre*, the aforementioned terrarium. Along with the snails, I also placed several half rounds of four-inch-long PVC pipe inside the terrarium. One held chicken feed, a supposed favorite of snails that I imagine they seldom get to indulge in (the possibility of a hungry chicken showing up just too likely). The other half rounds were piled on each other to provide shelter. The only other amenities were a very shallow water dish and a pile of greens (both of which I changed daily).

Right away there were problems. Who knew how much snails "evacuated?" I had to rinse out the unwieldy glass-sided terrarium every day and even that didn't seem quite enough. So then I put dirt in the aquarium, and worms, because worms eat snail poop. (Remind me not to eat worms.) That was better, but then came the problem of escape.

A snail can wedge itself into position, then push with a force equal to ten or more times its own weight. Get an entire snail crew that desire freedom (singing snail chanteys most likely), and their combined efforts can loosen nails and pop lids from their moorings.

The first time I noticed the lid askew and half the aquarium denizens AWOL, I figured I'd failed to push the metal lid—which had in other times kept proportionally giant geckos, tortoises, and mice successfully jailed—all the way down. The second time, I realized it was the snails. No wonder commercial snail farmers use electric fences to keep their livestock contained.

I went through the house rounding up the escaped doggies, which had left silver trails (not so easy to clean, by the way) up the walls, across the linoleum, along the countertops, and meandering around the appliances. While I spent a good amount of time on the hunt, I did not find them all. I knew there were snails lurking out of my sight because every morning I found cellulose-rich items such as mail, book pages, and newspapers, covered with large chew holes. Actually, the paper was not so much chewed as licked.

Snails eat by running what looks like a tongue (to the tongued, anyway) around the surface of its meal. The tongue is actually a *radula*— a muscular protuberance with teeth on it, worthy of a horror flick, that grinds away the snail's meal.

Constantly finding snail slicks across my appliances and having to explain my shredded checkbook to grocery checkers was bad enough.

When I squashed a snail in my bare feet during a 2:00 a.m. visit to the bathroom, I decided I couldn't keep the snails inside any longer.

Out in the goose yard, I stacked two raised wooden beds to make a tall box and planted chard and lettuce plants inside, salted the place with earthworms, and sunk a shallow dish for water. I moved all the snails into this new housing and bent a sheet of heavy wire mesh into a lid and weighted the top with several bricks, each of which I could hardly lift. Every day, I misted the produce and the snails with the hose, and Sunny patrolled the escargotierre with a hungry quacking, which seemed to dissuade any attempts at escape. By this time I had noticed that there were more snails in my escargotierre than there had been before; teeny tiny ones. My snails had procreated! Snails are as skilled at multiplying as they are at escape. While it does take *two* snails to do their reproductive tango, it can be *any* two snails. Snails are hermaphrodites, schlepping the equipment for both teams inside those shells of theirs. Mating ensues when there is at least eight hours of daylight and continues until days begin to get shorter. Five days to three weeks after mating, the designated "female" snail crawls partway into her nest (hole in the ground) and shoots out about eighty eggs (which hatch in two to four weeks) through the genital opening behind "her" head. The placement of the genital opening doesn't seem very well thought out, if you ask me, but then to a snail, the human situation may seem rather awkward as well.

For those with a great deal of patience, or a lot more snails, snail caviar flavored with a tincture of rosemary is supposed to be as much of a treat as escargot. Keep in mind that it takes 260 snails to lay enough caviar to make up a single kilogram.

I was not patient, but I did know how to procrastinate. Weeks were passing and I was getting worried my snails were going to be tired old retirees before I found the guts to cook 'em up. But snails actually have a pretty long life span, living up to five years. Snails don't even get the "lip" on their shell that signifies maturity for about nine months, so a few weeks was not going to push a snail past its prime. Even so, I needed to push ahead. It was time to eat the snails.

I dreaded killing the snails almost as much as I dreaded eating them. I tried not to think about it, but it was weighing on my mind. This was evident when I threw a party later that week for my friend Shawna Ryan and her novel debut of *Water Ghosts*. I made a special cookie cutter and cookies in her honor. The cookie was supposed to look like a moaning ghost rising from a coiling wave.

After I had made and frosted fifty of the ghost/wave cookies, Sam came in and pointed out that the cookies did not actually look like water ghosts, but crying snails instead. He was right—sobbing sugar-cookie snails with blue-frosted shells, to be exact. The prospect of doing the snails in was certainly weighing on me. I know it seems odd to worry about snail death considering that I made a practice of tossing them to the duck to gobble down. But in the duck's case, I figured any of the snail's discomfort at being swallowed by a duck was nature's responsibility. *My* killing them was a different situation altogether.

Perhaps Carl Jung was right in proposing that snails represented the self, with the soft subconscious encased in the hard outer shell of conscious thought; so perhaps I was identifying with the little guys. In that case, I decided to do them in by drowning the snails in beer. Snails, understandably, love beer. If you do not have ducks to keep your snail population in check in the garden, you might fill a shallow pan with even the cheapest beer (we call unpalatable beer "slug beer" at our house). Snails and slugs are drawn to the smell of yeast like frat boys to a keg party. They (and here I'm referring to snails and slugs) will plunge into beer with the abandon of pearl divers, never to crawl out again. (Unfortunately, snails and slugs love beer so much that it is possible this method could backfire, drawing these creatures instead from yards up and down your street with the scent of yeasty deliciousness.)

In any case, I hope that my snails' demise was easy. Whether it was, or especially if it wasn't, they got their revenge in the hours to come. After dunking them in the beer initially, I had to put the snails through another two washes because they "voided" when immersed in liquid. This would seem to be an indication that their end wasn't so good, but then again, maybe voiding in public was not a faux pas for snails like it is for even a horrendously drunk sports bar denizen.

Once I finished the three washes, I made another bath for the now dead snails, to which I added three tablespoons of salt and a half cup of vinegar. Now things really got bad—emanating from the dead snails were sounds like tiny snail flatulence or the mollusk equivalent of banshee wails. The water clouded, and when I changed it I clearly understood why we weren't all eating snails out of our gardens.

The amount of slime was unbelievable. Where was it all coming from? The mucilaginous glop draped across the surface of the water, adhered to the buckets and pans, and gloved onto my hands; I couldn't wash it off. I was revolted, and the last thing I could imagine doing at this point was putting any part of this mess into my mouth. I wondered if I could beg off the party; claim to suffer a migraine, the flu. But then, I fretted; I would be expected to reschedule.

I then feverishly imagined ways I could *appear* to eat snails but not really do so. Of course, I had the feeling my guests would all be watching me far too closely when I took the first bite of my homegrown escargot to successfully fake it.

So I pushed on, changing the water every fifteen minutes. Each time the slime was a little less voluminous, if still overwhelming. When the snails had been put through three water changes, the last rendering the water virtually slime-free, it was time to boil the snails.

To my chagrin, boiling the snails produced still *more* slime, and I tell you, cooked slime is no better than raw. What *was* this stuff issuing from the snails in such horrifying volume? How could one little snail produce so much glop? I was quite certain the volume of *slime* I was handling was larger than the volume of *snails* I was working with.

Snail (and slug) slime is a particularly intriguing substance once one gets past the shuddering. The reason there suddenly seemed like there was so much of it was because there *was* suddenly so much of it, even, just as I had fathomed, more slime than snail. Snails make their mucus out of dry granules of mucin that they carry around inside of them. When the dry granules come into contact with water and a small amount of calcium, they expand *six-hundred fold* into what we call slime in just forty milliseconds (which is the general amount of time it takes for a car's airbag to deploy).

The reason I couldn't wash the slime easily off my hands is because the thickness of the pedal mucus (as it comes from the "foot" of the snail) increases with the application of water. As I energetically tried to rinse the mucus from my skin, I was actually making the problem worse. The best thing to do if you are ever covered with snail mucus, say as a result of being pelted with slugs as a practical joke, or if you fall asleep nude in a snail-friendly garden one night, is to wipe it off with a dry paper towel or with a bit of vinegar. If, more likely, you find yourself with pedal mucus only on your hands, rub your hands together. The mucus will ball up as if it were rubber cement.

Then again, it might be wiser to revel in the mucus instead of fight it. Dab it onto your skin, massage it on your face. The many elements of snail slime (technically *Helix aspersa Müller* glycoconjugates) include glycoproteins, enzymes, and copper peptides that are said to improve skin texture and carry wound-healing abilities. Indeed, they found snail slime to be an effective treatment in the repair of radiodermatitis, or the skin damage that followed the Chernobyl Nuclear Power Plant disaster.

If the thought of letting a snail slime you "pedo-a-mano" makes you feel squeamish, you can purchase commercial snail-slime products including the lovely sounding facial lotion, *Crema de Caracal* (snail cream) or, following in the footsteps of eighteenth-century folk medicine—practicers who would swallow snails and slugs raw as a remedy for a weak chest—you can purchase Karacoflu, a snail-slime-based cough syrup that comes in either strawberry or avocado flavors.

Another potentially useful characteristic of snail slime is that it acts as both glue and lubricant. As such, it allows a snail to both crawl up walls and ceilings without toppling off, giving rise to one of the British terms for snails, "wall fish." Scientists are trying to create a synthetic version of snail slime for robots so they can climb walls and not topple off as well.

Once the snails were de-slimed, boiled, and cooled, I used a toothpick to jimmy the snail from its shell. This was not as easy as one would think, and I quickly found that it was easier to merely crush the shell and pull the meat from the shards. After I had a (somewhat soberingly) small pile of snail meat I—feeling like a colossus operating on a microbe—found and removed the teensy inedible parts of each tiny snail corpse. These parts I would describe as a "hard thing" and a "black thing." In scientific terms, that's cartilage and the intestinal tube. Once those were removed (and my pile of snail meat was that much smaller), I minced the meat and separated the snails into two piles. To one pile I added a mixture of parsley, butter, and garlic. To the other, a tomato-based mix of onion, anchovy, and cayenne. I took a small scooper and placed a perfect sphere of French snail or Spanish snail into the hollowed tops of mushrooms, which I placed on a divotted steel escargot dish ready to be set under the broiler when the guests had all arrived.

While Louis hunted and gathered the alcoholic beverages before everyone arrived, I had just enough time to put together the rest of the meal. With lots of wine and lots of non-snail food, as well as the two types of escargot, we were ready. I had a generous glass of red wine and sat down to wait for the friends I hoped would leave our house at the end of the evening feeling more like cherished guests than guinea pigs, or worse, victims. The guests included, at one end of the spectrum, three people who feel eating is, at its best, an adventure. They might be disappointed in the dinner, but they would avidly try it, and would unlikely be disgusted. At the other end of the spectrum were two people who had already said they would not be eating pets or pests that evening. The rest of us were cautious, but game enough that with the right lubrication (beer or wine), trying my snails wouldn't be an intolerable experience.

How was it? I have a photo Louis took that night that says everything. In it, two friends (one of the adventurers and one who had refused to eat snails) and I are caught mid chew. We are all eating the escargot. We all look giggly, slightly tipsy, slightly trepidatious, but happy; we look like we are having a great time. Moreover, *everyone* ate them. Including Louis. Sam even put two of the last snail-stuffed mushroom caps aside to take to school the next day (likely taking the prize for the fourteen-year-old with the most unusual lunch). That made all the slime wrangling worthwhile.

Escargot in Two Colors

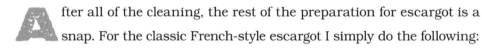fter all of the cleaning, the rest of the preparation for escargot is a snap. For the classic French-style escargot I simply do the following:

Ingredients for French-style Escargot:

- meat from 24 snails
- 24 white button mushrooms
- ½ cup softened butter
- 1 TB minced garlic
- ⅛ cup chopped parsley

1. Mince the garlic, finely chop the parsley, and mix both into the butter.

2. As I wait for the butter/parsley/garlic mixture to chill in the refrigerator, I clean my mushrooms. Even though I'm sure other types of mushrooms

might well be even more delicious, I used white button mushrooms because they had the most generously sized caps the day I purchased them.

3. I pull the stems from the caps and put them aside to use as stuffing for the mushroom caps that the snail-squeamish guests would eat.

4. From my pile of cleaned, cooked, and chopped snails, I take what seems to be a snail's worth of meat, stick it in the mushroom cap, and then with a melon baller, I scoop out a half globe of butter/parsley/garlic mix and place it on top of the snail meat inside the mushroom cap.

5. I put the filled caps on my snail dishes, which are stainless steel plates with divots in them to hold the snail-filled snail shells, or in this case, snail-stuffed mushrooms.

With several of the French-style escargot plates filled, it was time to move on to making the tomato-based snail recipe.

Ingredients for Spanish-style Escargot:
- meat from 24 snails
- 24 white button mushrooms
- 3 anchovy filets
- 2 cups reconstituted sun-dried tomatoes

- 2 TB olive oil
- ½ an onion, diced
- ⅛ tsp cayenne pepper
- salt to taste

1. Dissolve the anchovy filets in the olive oil.

2. Add diced onion and sauté until the onion is translucent.

3. Add cayenne pepper, and salt to taste, then transfer the onion/anchovy mixture into the food processor with the sun-dried tomatoes and puree into a paste.

4. Add snail meat to cleaned mushroom caps, but this time top the snails with a half globe of tomato/onion/anchovy mixture, then put them on still more divoted snail plates.

5. Sprinkle toasted bread crumbs over the tops of all the caps, and when your guests are happy with wine, conversation, and song, put the plates under the broiler on low (about ten minutes) until the food is bubbling hot.

This makes a great small-dish centered dinner. Along with the snails, I also served home-cured olives, fava beans with shaved pecorino, stuffed chard rolls, fennel celery salad, and baby beets with goat cheese. Except for the cheese, the food, like the snails, hearkened from the Quarter Acre Farm. Which got me thinking, I was so good at snail wrangling, how much more work could a goat be? (Just kidding, Louis)

MUMMIFICATION: THE ART OF CURING OLIVES

"They are twisted, they kneel to pray, and they raise their arms, members tyrannized by movement, all elbows and knees. The bent roots suck the golden oil from the heart of the earth for the lamps of the saints and the salad of the poor."
—STRATIS MYRIVILLIS, GREEK POET

I have no doubt that as scientists explore the genome, they will eventually map the location of the gene that compels children to stick their fingers into California-style pitted black olives so that their hands resemble the suction-cupped paws of a salamander, at which point, after no little waving of said paws, they then eat the olives one after the other like an epicurean king kissing crumbs from each fingertip.

It will likely be the same gene responsible for the fact that some children's fingers spend half their time lodged in one nostril or the other. I have a photograph of four-year-old Jesse standing on a riser with a construction paper mortarboard and tassel seated on his head, a finger in his nose. His teachers presented the photograph to me on the day of his preschool graduation (along with one in which they'd compelled him to let his nose go solo by clasping his hands in front of him), saying, "We just loved this one, it is so typical." (Jesse would like me to clarify that he has *long* since refrained from sticking his finger in his nose).

I don't know what happened to the latter picture with the clasped hands, but the former is in our photo album. It has character—unlike "ripe" canned black olives. Other than the perfectly sized hole, the draw of those olives lies in their blandness, a cool, slightly meaty taste overlaid with a metallic tang that might be attributable to the iron gluconate used to dye the olives black.

As a kid, I thought the California-style olives were so much better (as well as more entertaining) than the green olives—once you sucked the pimento out of it like a lamprey from it's undersea crevice, all that was left was a hole too small for a finger and the bitter green fruit that, yes, tasted like it wasn't ripe yet.

Were it not for my Italian Grandmother, I would have thought those two varieties encompassed the entire, unimpressive olive world. But she happened to marry a Greek man, who would every so often bring Greek olives to our house. These my father would declaim as unfit for eating, but my mother would eat them with great relish out of sight of my father.

The bizarre things my mother ate before she married my father and learned to cook like my father's mother, in the German/English tradition, were a litany in our house. Not only had she consumed those weirdly shriveled olives, but also brown butter on spaghetti, anchovies, and baked *bananas*, for Pete's sake. We felt sorry for her.

I apologize now for the sneering. Browned butter (especially simmered with a handful of sage leaves tossed in until crisp) over pasta is delicious. Anchovies, along with salt and pepper, should be considered as an indispensable seasoning. Baked bananas? Bring them on! And Greek olives make practically everything better.

Especially *my* Greek olives.

When we moved to our current house, one of the best things about it was the enormous olive tree growing in the backyard. It had a wide grey-green canopy supported by gnarled reaching limbs, all elbows and knees. It produced thousands of thumb-sized olives that when ripe were deep purple-black obscured with a slight haze. Buff the cloud away and pinprick stars shone on the gleaming surface. For years I did nothing with the olives other than sweep them off the patio we built under the tree, hoping to keep the family from tracking the oily fruit into the house.

Then I noticed groups of urban gleaners picking the olives off trees that lined one of the main throughways in Davis, and from the trees overhanging the bike paths further out of town. I asked the pickers what they did with the olives. For most of the people I talked to, English was not their first language, and though they did a *lot* better with their second language than I did with mine (faint praise unintended), it took some doing to get their ideas across. I appreciated the efforts since what these people did with their olives was wonderfully varied.

Some soaked them in water, changing the baths each day; others soaked their olives in saltwater brine, which seemed to require a less frequent soaking-solution change. There were gleaners who used ashes to treat their olives, and one guy who said he had a yearly tradition of salting the olives in December, then pitting them as he watched the Super Bowl a month or so later.

I described my tree and the fruit it produced to another gleaner who was a longtime Davis resident. He gave me an envious look. "There was a tree just like that out by Bee Biology Road. Huge olives, and they were good." He shook his head. "They cut it down."

Olives come in more varieties than apples trees do, having been in cultivation for thousands of years longer. Their fruit, or drupes, have been encouraged toward different uses: oil, canning, or dual purpose. The *grades* of oil, however, came from the method of production (the old method of pressing on grass mats) with the best oil being extra virgin. The final pressing of the dregs produced an oil called "lampante," that was used for lamp fuel.

While in most instances an expert can identify a tree by the fruit of the olive, the most reliable identification is done by examining the ridges in the pit, each variety exhibiting different ridging characteristics.

The fruit of an olive tree is born on one-year-old wood, so each year the olives' fruit rises farther out of reach. Olive producers rectify this by severely pruning the tree, curtailing its height and encouraging new lower growth that can be reached by workers. When the olives are ripe, workers beat the heck out of the tree branches with long sticks and special rakes, dislodging olives onto tarps spread at the foot of the tree.

This method, however, has drawbacks. Not only may it damage the tree, but it can also damage the fruit, which starts to oxidize as a wound response. This oxidization makes for a less than perfect olive oil which is why growers such as Mike Madison from Yolo Press take the time to pick their fruit gently by hand.

If the olive grower has a big spread—some Greek orchards have over a million trees—they are less likely to utilize the hands-on approach. They might use pneumatic rakes, harvesters with rotating fiberglass rods, or a machine that is aptly called a "shaker" to gather their olives (my favorite being the one that starts it's work by elegantly unfurling a tarp at the base of the tree like a frilled lizard unfolding its neck cape). It grabs the tree by the trunk with a mechanical arm and shakes the olives from the branches, removing 80 to 90 percent of the fruit in about fifteen seconds. I can't help but wonder if anyone has ever grabbed something other than a tree with that machine. Imagine what it could do with ice cream and milk.

In Chile, Argentina, and Australia, they have a machine called the Colossus, which drives over the full-size olive trees and knocks off the fruit. I imagine the driver of the behemoth machine intoning the inscription from the original Colossus (an ancient 110-foot-tall statue so big that two men could hardly touch fingers when reaching around the girth of the thumb): "Not only over the seas but also on land did thy kindle the lovely torch of freedom . . ." Perhaps fitting since olive oil has fueled lamps for thousands of years.

My own tree had not been pruned for at least twenty years, perhaps longer, effectively making the tree into what an olive grower would call a "feral" tree. The olive production had slowed, and the olives it did produce hung precariously high. Still, it was dropping enough olives every year for my personal use.

Therefore, it was time to do something with my wonder olives. I went to the campus bookstore and picked up a pamphlet detailing lye curing, brine curing, and salt curing olives. At the bottom of the page was the author's name, the one-time olive specialist at UC Davis, the late Reese Vaughn.

Reese Vaughn?! He and his family had owned our house for almost half a century before we had bought it. *He* must have been the one to plant our tree. I imagined our tree to be the equivalent of the magic beanstalk, perhaps the result of a seed Mr. Vaughn had found in the midden of an ancient orchard site. Fossilized olive seeds had been found in Crete that carbon dated to 3,500 years old, and while one obviously can't sprout a fossilized seed, there was a tree in Crete that through tree-ring calculations was estimated to be 2,000 years old. In fact, it is said that the olive tree that grows near the temple of Athena, the Erechtheion at the Acropolis, is the very first olive tree, sprouting there after Athena struck her spear into the ground. Thus, not only were olives birthed, but Athens was as well. Perhaps Reese had brought back one of Athena's olives and the progeny was in our backyard!

Goddess tree or no, I was avid to cure my olives, and the method that appealed to me most was salt curing. It was the most straightforward way, for one thing, but it was also a form of mummification. And I knew mummification.

Sam was an ancient civilizations buff from the age of three. Every night for two years we read Sue Clarke's *The Tombs of The Pharoahs* to him along with passages from more scholarly tomes. When he was four, I caught on that he was reading cartouches in order to identify the pharaoh who was buried in a particular pyramid. When Sam was nine, I made him an Anubis costume, the jackal-headed God of the underworld and eater of unjust hearts, for Halloween.

The point being, a few years into Sam's lifelong love of the ancient world, I became pretty darn informed about ancient Egypt. I figured that if I were somehow sent back in time and was called upon to act as an ancient Egyptian priest, I could weasel the brain from a pharaoh's nasal passages, flop his internal organs into canopic jars, and dehydrate what was left of the fellow with natron, no problem.

With olives, there was no brain weaseling, no organ flopping, just basic mummification. A piece of cake.

The salt used in mummification, be it for Pharaohs or olives, not only dehydrates the flesh but also makes the situation within the olive's "meat" inhospitable to bacteria. No liquid, no bacteria, no rot.

The first time I cured my olives, I layered my olives and salt in cardboard boxes. The trouble with cardboard is that the olives release a goodly amount of liquid as they cure (not only water but the bitter tasting, albeit stellar antioxidant, chemical compound oleuropein.) The bottom of the boxes became sodden and the whole project teetered on the edge of falling apart, a great deal messier than it had to be.

For the next batch, I made a beautiful peg-joined, hinged-top pine box into which I drilled hundreds of holes for aeration. Into this box I layered salt and olives, thinking of the time, perhaps hundreds of years in the future, in which this pine box might still be used for olive curing by the children of my children's children, the lovely patina of olive oil and salt marking its century-old planks.

Unfortunately, while the box was sturdy, I found there was no truly effective way to press down the salt within the box. While the olives desiccated and shrank, tiny caves formed around the fruit, and where the olive flesh was not in contact with the salt, molding occurred.

With the third batch, I abandoned my no longer useful heirloom-worthy box and used a less romantic but much more utilitarian plastic burlap bag instead. Within the bag I layered bulk sea salt, then a layer of washed ripe olives, followed by more sea salt and more olives, until the bag was over half full. I tied the top closed then stood it in a large plant saucer—which I emptied when the olive "juices" collected there.

In addition, every day or so I rolled the plastic burlap bag full of salt and olives about, effectively shaking up the salt and collapsing those salt caves around the olives. It worked like a charm. At the end of six to eight weeks, when the olives were shriveled and no longer tasted wicked bitter but deep and warm, I separated the olives from the salt, packed the olives in Ziploc bags, then froze them.

When I needed olives, I took a bag from the freezer, rinsed the remnant salt from the olives, and packed them in a canning jar with cloves of garlic, sprigs of rosemary, a piece of hot pepper, and perhaps some basil. I heated olive oil and poured it over the olives and herbs, then stuck the jar of olives, herbs, and oil in the refrigerator. After a week, they were ready to use.

Unlike the guy who pitted his olives watching the Super Bowl, I don't pit mine until I'm ready to use them. I use a hand-held cherry pitter and pop out the pits, then cut up the olives to use in focaccia, on pizza, or in tomato sauce, or I eat them plain. The deep warm umami taste is the perfect counterpoint for the tangy tomato sauces, the heat of chile peppers, or soft bread dough fragrant with rosemary. Heavenly. Of course, Athena *is* the goddess of wisdom. She knew what she was doing.

Olive Focaccia

Focaccia is delicious, gorgeous, and a whole host of other "ous-es" too numerous to mention here. Focaccia is also easy to make and if you "proof" your yeast (a must-do, especially if you don't make bread often), not much can go wrong.

Why proof the yeast? The poor yeast could have expired in the long cold winter of your refrigerator. How do you proof? Add your yeast to a bit of slightly warm water, mix in a tablespoon each of flour and sugar, and you'll soon learn if it is viable. Within fifteen minutes, live yeast will become good and bubbly. Dead yeast will merely drift to the bottom of your bowl like sludge, and sit there.

Kneading will tell you when you've got good dough on your hands. The dough should feel stretchy with a bit of snap, like it has an opinion about its own shape. Once the dough is in good shape, don't stint on the rising.

As it rises, yeast is multiplying through a process called budding—new yeast cells bud off the old ones. This process produces enzymes that change the starch in the flour to sugar, then change the sugar into alcohol and carbon dioxide. During rising, the carbon dioxide makes holes. During baking, the alcohol evaporates and makes for even more holes and lighter bread.

Obviously you do not want to stymie the yeast's work. Not only do you want light bread, but you also want the flavors that are being formed from the starches changing to sugar and sugars to alcohol.

Ingredients:

- 2 TB yeast
- 4 cups flour
- 2 cups warm water
- ¼ cup (⅛ cup chopped) pitted olives
- 2 TB olive oil (plus a little extra for brushing on the focaccia)
- 1 TB fresh rosemary
- salt
- 1 tablespoon each of flour and sugar for proofing

1. Proof the yeast by mixing it with the water.

2. When it is foaming, add the olive oil and as much flour as it takes to make a slightly sticky wad of dough.

3. Dust the dough with flour and knead the dough for around 10 to 15 minutes. (If you've got a mixer with a dough hook it makes it easier, though lots of people like kneading the dough by hand.)

4. After the dough is kneaded, put it into a bowl, cover it with a towel, and let it expand for up to two hours. It will enlarge faster in the summer than the winter, especially if you live in a house in which the builders apparently forgot to install insulation, like mine.

5. When the dough is all puffed up with itself, it's time to take charge and impress upon it your own desires. Punch the dough down and knead it a bit, then roll/press it into any shape *you* think fit, but about an inch thick. I do my rolling/pressing on a sheet of parchment paper, which I can then transfer, paper and all, to a cookie sheet when I'm ready to bake.

6. After your dough is pressed, cut your pitted olives in half and press them into the dough. You can use any kind of pitted olives, even green ones.

7. I also chop fresh rosemary and press that into dimples in the dough, then generously brush the top of the rapidly rising focaccia with olive oil and sprinkle with flaked sea salt.

8. Allow to rise until double, then put the focaccia into the 350 degree oven until it is golden brown (about 25 to 30 minutes).

This is great as is or dipped in balsamic vinegar and olive oil)—or try inside out sandwiches, as follows:

1. Slice the cooled bread into sandwich-sized pieces, and then cut the pieces horizontally into a top and a bottom.

2. Butter the inside surfaces of the bread and heat your panini grill. The inside buttered pieces will now be facing out, touching the grill, so that the evenly cut soft bread will get toasted.

3. On the bumpy inside (with the olives) put slices of cheese, such as havarti, and perhaps some sliced chicken or salami or hard boiled egg, and some roasted red pepper. Grill.

4. After the sandwich is browned and the cheese melted, remove the sandwich to a plate and put a leaf of fresh lettuce and even a slab of peppered tomato inside.

Beauteous. Fabulous. Glorious. Ravenous?

THE HISTORY OF FOOD PRESERVATION, INCLUDING MY OWN

"Of course I can!"
—U.S. FOOD ADMINISTRATION POSTER, 1944

Pre-history: A frozen seal on the ice. It's simple to see where the idea of using cold as a preservative came from; some prehistoric someone noticed that frozen seal didn't *smell* unpalatable like the one they'd dragged inside by the fire.

As well as being the most straightforward method of preserving food, freezing also has the most documented success. In 1984, paleontologists Bjorn Kurten and Dale Guthrie actually ate *Bison priscus* meat after it had been frozen in Alaska for 36,000 years. Bjorn wrote that the meat, when thawed, "gave off an unmistakable beef aroma, not unpleasantly mixed with a faint smell of the earth in which it was found, with a touch of mushroom . . . the taste was delicious." Dale Guthrie, however, intimated that it wasn't entirely wonderful when he described his meal as giving off a strong *Pleistocene* aroma, which I can't imagine would be terribly appetizing.

Freezing food has its limits. The water molecules in the food form ice crystals as they freeze, but these water molecules try to find the best environment in which to den up for their frozen winter. That best environment for an ice crystal wanna-be is the coldest place available, which is often outside of the food. (The side of the freezer seems to be the Club Med for ice crystals.) Once enough water molecules have abandoned ship, the food becomes somewhat dehydrated, or "freezer burned." As if that isn't bad enough, the dearth of water molecules provides opportunity for oxygen molecules to sneak in, which also change the appearance and taste of the food.

Beyond freezer burn, there are plenty of bacteria that act on foods at temperatures below freezing as well. In short, if you happen to come across a frozen mastodon, I wouldn't recommend eating it. Of course, I may worry overmuch about such things.

When I was in junior high I used to go to my best friend's house and feel great trepidation at the fact that they used their screened porch as a freezer. It was Wyoming and Thanksgiving-time, but it just seemed dangerous to cart the turkey, gravy, stuffing, and cranberry sauce out to the picnic table and *leave* it there until someone got a hankering for a sandwich and carted it all back in again. For one thing, I knew the temperature must fluctuate out there from well below freezing to a sunny 45 degrees, but also my friend had a big tomcat named McGregor.

One might think a cat wouldn't be interested in frozen food, and to them I offer the story of the mule deer that a hunter hung in a tree a hundred yards from the trailer I lived in during my early twenties. The hunter had skinned the carcass and hung it to cool, intending to cut it up later. The hunter procrastinated, the deer froze, and over the next two months I watched as ranch cats clung to the swaying venison popsicle, gnawing on the flesh.

One trouble with freezing food in most parts of the world, pre-artificial-cold era, was that the weather wasn't likely to be cold enough to freeze food when much food was available to freeze. And once the weather did get cold, there was no certainty that it would stay cold. To combat this problem, ice was packed into cellars and insulated with straw to keep things cold for as long as the ice lasted. In a small step forward, or maybe sideways, people in China, circa the fourth century, noticed that evaporating salt water was cold and that containers with food in them placed in the brine would keep things chilled.

Some centuries later, a Glaswegian by the name of William Cullen figured out the theory of artificial refrigeration, followed by an American inventor who figured out how to make a refrigeration *machine* in 1834. John Gorrie, an American physician, took things another step forward and made a refrigerat*or* in order to make ice to cool his yellow-fever patients.

How does refrigeration work? Liquid is compressed, and compressed liquids evaporate into vapor. The rapidly expanding vapor requires energy to expand and so draws the energy from the immediate area—in our case, the inside of the refrigerator box. The refrigerator box loses energy and so grows cooler.

To understand all this, it helps to remember that there isn't really any cold. What we call cold is merely the absence of heat. This is a difficult idea for me as I imagine cold like a stalker, always breathing down my neck, waiting for me around the corner, lingering in between the sheets, and coiling around my feet. Cold isn't an entity, however. Cold doesn't grow; *heat escapes.* Therefore, I am not being stalked, I am merely being abandoned.

Clarence Birdseye brought one of the next big inventions in refrigeration history into the world. He found that metal plates soaked in calcium chloride brine and chilled (shades of fourth-century China) could quickly freeze foods sandwiched between those plates. Thereafter frozen food became increasingly popular, to the point that many children and even adults believed that corn kernels, peas, and cubed carrots all grew on the same plant.

At the Quarter-Acre Farm, while I have no flash-freezing capabilities, I rely on freezing to preserve much of the food I grow for later. We freeze our food in the small chest-freezer our neighbors lent us. It is big enough that (in theory) a full-grown man could be folded inside with some effort, if (creepily) necessary. It holds just enough produce for our family of three to get us through the winter, and once again I get by with a little help from my friends.

I freeze roasted tomato sauce, roasted tomatoes, fresh cherry tomatoes, roasted eggplant, figs, fig puree, chopped fruit, pesto, green chile, and sweet peppers. I also use the freezer to store dried foodstuffs, especially the dried tomatoes that I like a little chewy rather than entirely desiccated. Freezing nuts keeps them from becoming rancid or a target for mealy worms.

What might be more important than what I do freeze is what I don't freeze. I try *never* to freeze fruit juice. Not because it doesn't freeze well, but because it does. I've had grape juice taunt me for well over a year. "You lazy excuse for a farmer, I thought you were going to make jelly last month. But no, you were *too busy*. Too busy now as well after all the energy that it's taken to keep me frozen for an eternity? Yeah, too busy checking Facebook maybe." It's misery, and if you let it get to you, the shame of eventually throwing it away could keep you from farming altogether.

I also try not to freeze large amounts in one bag. A giant peach boulder is so difficult to work with it is likely to become garbage before it has a chance to be made into pie. Therefore I have learned to make everything I put in the freezer (immediately) user friendly. Sauce is frozen in one-meal servings. Enough chiles are frozen per bag to make one pot of green-chile stew. I roast cubes of eggplant, spread them on a cookie sheet to freeze, then put them into bags so I can sprinkle eggplant on pizza or pour it into stew or between sheets of noodles for lasagna. Fruit is frozen in the same way so that a cup of peaches can easily be put into smoothies or four cups into pies. Zucchini is grated, then pressed with a potato ricer to get rid of excess water. I put the resulting pucks on the cookie sheet to freeze, and the frozen pucks are bagged and put in the chest freezer until I need a couple for mid-December zucchini fritters or to puree with tomato soup. Cherry tomatoes are picked straight into a bag and tossed into the freezer.

Interestingly enough, the freezer seems the realm of summer produce. Winter fruit and vegetables do not seem to come ready all at once, and when they are ready they can bide their time a bit better out in the cold garden waiting to be picked.

I try to have the freezer empty by the time the first tomatoes are coming on and full by the time the last tomatoes are finishing up. If I manage that, I know I will be able to eat well all winter long and into the spring.

Like freezing, dehydrating is a naturally occurring event. Drying as a means of preservation has been practiced at least since 12,000 BC, first in the Middle East. Initially, it only required people to notice that, "Hey, those dried grapes never even molded and they taste pretty darn good." Later, Vikings air dried their fish in the riggings of their ships. Many Native American tribes took it a step further and pounded dried meat with fat and fruit resulting in a food called pemmican.

Drying was such a good idea that in the Middle Ages people in places that didn't have an environment conducive to dehydrating food set up "still houses," where the heat from fires (and likely the smoke as well) dried and preserved meat, fruit, and vegetables.

Dehydrating food, as the name suggests, removes the moisture needed for decomposition. Food without moisture is also lighter in weight, smaller, and so requires less storage space. It intensifies the taste of foods, and even changes the character of the taste. The change in taste is the primary reason I can be found on most summer mornings slicing fruits and vegetables onto the trays of my dehydrator.

Dried tomatoes are *so* good. So good on pizza, in stews, tossed in pasta. Adding boiling water to dried tomatoes then pureeing makes for the most delicious tomato paste ever. A little more water and it becomes the most delicious tomato sauce ever. Take that sauce and add chopped dried tomatoes for a wonderful double-tomato tomato sauce. To *that* add some of those frozen cubes of roasted eggplant, and some onions, and you're about to enter the state of nirvana. You will remember summer even in mid-January.

My mother once dehydrated watermelon. It is worth doing once (on a silicone mat or parchment paper) just for the sense of how much of watermelon is water. The resulting leather is not as good as watermelon, so I wouldn't do it twice. My mother also dehydrates other fruits, most notably the Prairie Spy apples she tosses with cinnamon and sugar and sends me every year for Christmas. They are better than chocolate. *Really.*

Pears are the most changed of the dehydrated fruits. I don't care for fresh pears. They are grainy and have an unpleasant, oddly leathery skin. But dehydrated pears are transformed into a lush, chewy deliciousness. I didn't believe that could happen to a pear, but my friend Joannie convinced me to give it a try and I am forever grateful.

Fermentation is the next on our food preservation time-line. Fermentation utilizes microorganisms to preserve food such as grains, hops, and cabbage. Beer has been made since 10,000 BC. Kimchi and sauerkraut, which are the Korean and German variations on cabbage, are two more examples of fermented foods. I have not delved into this. I had a friend who made kimchi in her refrigerator once and while I *dearly* love kimchi, I would have to have a dedicated kimchi refrigerator (which Samsung does make, by the way), or perhaps a dedicated kimchi room, to attempt making it due to the sinus-clearing pungency of the fermenting cabbage.

Though I don't ferment on the Quarter-Acre Farm (not on purpose, anyway), I *do* pickle. Pickling is preserving food through the use of acid. When I was a kid, a pickle meant a dill pickle. The best pickle was the elusive "dill teeny" (out of Wyoming such a pickle is known as a cornichon), which only seemed available during the holiday season. The second-best pickle was on the other end of the pickle spectrum: a gigantic pickle in a gigantic jar on the counters of family-owned grocery stores. My Grandma Streeter would take us to one such market where I couldn't understand how everyone seemed to know her name. *My* parents shopped at Safeway, where everyone wore the same corporate smock and to whom we were absolutely anonymous.

At the family market my Grandma would treat us to pickles wrapped in a sheet of translucent paper that we'd peel like a banana. We'd bite the top off the salty, sharp-tasting pickle, and suck the soft-seeded insides out until the pickle "husk" was wrinkled as dog lips. I couldn't always finish such a monumental pickle, so the vinegary remnants were sadly tossed in the trash.

My mother made watermelon pickles, which looked, smelled, and tasted nothing like pickles or watermelon. I didn't like them much. For one thing, pickles should be vinegary/salty, not sweet, and it ruined the watermelon eating experience as well. While it's only the rind that's pickled, my mother felt it was important to leave a layer of red watermelon on the rind to make the "pickles" look pretty. With regular watermelon, we kids liked to eat the rind all the way to the green, the tangy pale crunchiness a pleasant counterpoint to the sweet red flesh, and we certainly didn't want to miss any of the red flesh.

But my mother would hover, nagging us about the correct amount of fruit to leave. It was worse when she trimmed the rind off the watermelon *before* giving us the fruit, for while that saved us from her hovering, we'd have to use a fork and plate to eat watermelon, and that just isn't right.

I don't make watermelon pickles at the Quarter-Acre Farm, though I think I'd enjoy them now. All my watermelon rinds go to the geese. It would be impossible for us to enjoy watermelon pickles even half as much as Jeannette and Goosteau enjoy those rinds. When we throw the rinds over the goose fence, Jeannette runs so fast she hovers on airborne. Goosteau brings up the rear with a little more dignity, reflecting a sad bout of bumblefoot that has made him more cautious about tripping and injuring his feet. Once they've put beak to rind, however, both of them burst into delightful burbling that we refer to as "the pleasure noise." It is so gratifying to elicit such a tickled response in our rather ill-tempered geese that we have been known to buy them an entire watermelon for special events, like Goosteau's birthday or summer solstice.

I have pickled plums at the Quarter Acre Farm, but since I don't like pickled plums it wasn't such a good idea. On the other hand, I love fresh cucumbers so much there are never enough of them to pickle. At the end of the season, however, there are always plenty of green to-matoes. The green cherry tomatoes are especially nice when pickled. They're also quite pretty speared and floating in a martini, and they are chewier than cucumber pickles. I often eat an entire jar full just for the fun of biting them (and then am sorry for it; a jar of vinegary/salty pick-les is at least half a jar too much). They are the spherical equivalent of dill teenies.

Most pickles are not only pickled but canned. Which brings us to 1790, when a French confectioner discovered that applying heat to sealed containers discouraged the contamination of food. It was thought that the exclusion of air was responsible for the good effects, and it wasn't until 1864, when Louis Pasteur figured out the relationship between microorganisms and food spoilage, that the full truth was known.

Canning, as the name suggests, was originally done in cans—hand-made wrought-iron tin cans, to be exact. The cans were so expensive to make and the canning so laborious that canned food became a status symbol among middle-class people in Europe. Imagine a dinner party, the best china and your mother's silver on the table. With all the guests seated, you . . . open a can of Beanie Weenies.

Cost wasn't the only problem. The seams of the cans, as well as the lids, were soldered with lead, leading to some disastrous consequences. The 1847 Franklin Expedition to the Canadian Arctic took thousands of canned goods with them on their journey. The ill-fated crew never returned, and it took over a hundred years before modern toxicology reports on the victims' hair and bone samples revealed levels of lead in their systems a hundred times higher than is considered acceptable.

When double-seamed cans were invented in 1900, the dangers of lead poisoning were diminished. (Though, shockingly, lead solder in food cans was not outlawed in the United States until 1984.)

Texas Dairyman Gail Borden developed techniques to prepare evaporated and sweetened condensed milk so that it could be brought to market in cans. Carnation milk followed, which gave rise to the cowboy poem:

Carnation milk
The best in the land
Here I sit with a can in my hand
No tits to pull
No hay to pitch
Just poke a hole in the son of a bitch.

In 1858, John L. Mason invented the now famous Mason canning jar, and homemakers the world over began to preserve food using the jars with a zinc lid and rubber seal.

Home canning is a famously labor-intensive job. You not only need to clean, trim, chop, mix, and flavor the food that you're jarring (on the Quarter-Acre Farm, it is usually jelly, chutney, jam, marmalade, or pickles), but you also have to process the jars of food, which can be time consuming. This is why canning has so often been a) a job attempted only once or b) a cooperative sport.

If you can face canning a second time, you'll find it gets easier. One of my favorite books when I was a kid was *Cheaper by the Dozen*, the story of efficiency experts Frank and Lillian Gilbreth and their twelve children. This book is not to be confused with the awful Disney film that has but one saving grace—showing that even comic masters like Steve Martin can make mistakes.

What I loved about the original book was the application of "motion studies" on family life, how the father figured out how to take the best bath with the least number of movements and the smallest amount of time. "You take the soap in the left hand . . ." He mapped out the journey of the soap over the body. Brilliant. (Louis finds my appreciation of an efficient bath regimen rather strange because I myself am a *soaker* and usually meet the idea of hurrying out of steaming water with no little incredulity.) Frank Gilbreth figured out ways to make use of all sorts of wasted time *and* wasted space (as long as one is sitting on the loo staring at a blank wall, why not stare at *fill in the blank* instead and learn something). If we could all learn the best way to do something, we would have huge amounts of time to dedicate to other pursuits.

I've found that the more you practice, the more you'll learn the ideal way to prepare food. That's why it is so much fun to watch celebrity cooks like Mario or Yan or Julia on the tube. Mostly, there's no dithering, researching how to peel a cactus paddle, calling your mom for instructions, cleaning up the flour spilled all over the floor, or bandaging sliced fingers. Just expert measuring, mixing, and magical high-speed knife work that results in culinary masterworks in the space of half an hour.

That said, there's nothing like an entire tree full of ripe fruit to act as stern taskmaster overseeing your passage from novice to expert in cutting up a bunch of produce.

The first couple of years after we planted our fruit trees, there was no need to wonder about how we were going to use all the excess fruit we had. The family, usually standing directly under the tree where fruit tastes the very, very best, easily consumed all of the fruit. By the third and fourth years of our trees' lives, however, enough fruit ripened that we would have to do something about it or risk letting it go to waste (a moral failing in my book).

The first big producer was our purple plum tree. Louis helped me pick the fruit and then he fled the house. Good thing, because after spending about an hour trying to cut the flesh from the pit (plums are *not* freestone), and hardly making a dent in the pile, I was not happy, I'd cut myself twice, and I was wasting the fruit that clung to the top and bottom of the pit.

My speed, however, improved the second hour, and by my third hour chopping plums, I was so fast I could have chopped another tree-full of plums in half the time it had taken me to chop the first. I had discovered the secret to cutting up fruit-in-which-flesh-clings-to-the-pit.

Cut the fruit all the way to the pit, all the way around, like slicing an equator into the fruit. Twist the fruit apart. Half of the fruit will then have a pit, the other will be clean. Cut the piece of fruit in half to the pit again. Twist again. This will result in two quarter pieces of fruit, one without the pit and one with. Most of the time you can then take hold of the pit and twist it cleanly off. If not, make one more equatorial cut and one more twist.

To make the process even faster, make all of the first equatorial cuts then do the entire first twists, then all of the second cuts and the second twists. Just as there is a best way to de-pit a plum, there is a best way for almost every chore. You either have to be taught that best way or, unfortunately, figure it out for yourself. But when you do, it goes fast.

To figure out the best and fastest way to process a tree full of fruit, *get help.*

It's safe to say that cooperative work has probably been around as long as there has been work to do. Certainly in modern American history, the idea of sharing work—either out of necessity (it is a tad difficult to raise a barn on your own) or because it's more efficient (and sociable) (threshing, corn husking)—is woven into the fabric of our culture.

When food shortages became a part of American life, households were called upon to grow as much of their own food as possible so that the *commercially* grown produce could be sent to the soldiers fighting in WWII. Citizens started gardening in a big way. By 1944, food production was 38 percent above the national average of 1935-39 because fifteen million families planted gardens. In 1942 and '43, twenty million gardens produced 40 percent of the vegetables grown for home consumption. Canning was an important part of the war effort. The Committee on Food Supply and Conservation exhorted women to preserve food through canning. Women put up almost 10,000 jars of jelly and vegetables and husked and dried over 30,000 ears of corn. The burden of work was lightened as women got together to share their labors, and while sharing the job of canning, they also built a community where they could socialize, share common experiences and worries, enjoy conviviality, and educate the less experienced among them on how to preserve food.

Cooperative work is not exclusive to America, in any way. In societies all over the globe, cooperative work is common. Anthropologist William Bascomb points out that in West Africa, Yuba people even have distinct words to describe different types of work sharing. For example, one word connotes a simple labor exchange while another describes a group working together in much the same way as a barn-raising. Other cultures do their work in concert with singing or drumming so that rows of weeding or planting are finished at the same time. And almost all cooperative work is wrapped up by sharing food and drink.

There is a reason that the cooperative work is *wrapped up* this way and not offered mid effort.

After I'd figured out the secret to plum pitting, the green plums came ripe. My friend Sally was game to come over and make plum butter with me. I demonstrated the Spring-method of plum pitting and we got to work. There were a lot of plums, and we had started late in the afternoon—really, it was practically evening. Late enough that it seemed a good idea to have a shot of particularly nice single-malt scotch to encourage our good work. Perhaps not surprisingly, the single malt had the opposite effect. The first basket of plums were stoned and diced in short order, but the second took quite a bit longer, and by the time Louis got home, Sally and I had each sliced open a finger or two and decided that we didn't really want to cut up plums. I had to finish the plum butter by myself, fingers clumsily bandaged, the next day.

After a hot day spent water-bathing jars incessantly, a home-canner is usually tired and sticky and doesn't want to eat anything. If this happens to you, just remember all the fruit you've been freezing as well, because now's the perfect time to enjoy it by making a smoothie.

Smoothies

We drink a lot of smoothies at our house. In the summertime I have them for breakfast, lunch, and . . . if I could stand all the complaining from my family, for dinner as well.

Ingredients:

▶ 1 cup fresh or frozen fruit of your choice

▶ ¼ cup Greek (I like Vanilla) yogurt

   or 2-3 TB protein powder

   or ½ banana

▶ water or juice to thin smoothie consistency if necessary

1. If you've got fresh fruit, toss the washed, pitted, de-stemmed fruit (plums, strawberries, blueberries, peaches, apricots) into a blender with ice cubes and turn it on. This makes a frothy cold drink but lacks a little smoothie substance.

2. I like to add a banana, some Greek yogurt, or protein powder to give it what I (possibly weirdly) think of as *taste opacity*. Others might call it creaminess.

Of course, the best smoothies are made from frozen fruit because not only can you use June strawberries (or May apricots, for that matter) well into the rest of the year when they might not otherwise be available, but you also don't have to add ice cubes. Ice cubes not only water down the flavor of the smoothie, but when you puree them, it sounds more like you're crushing rocks in the blender than concocting something edible.

How you freeze your fruit is going to make the difference in loving to make smoothies or hating it. I have found that the best way to freeze fruit of all kinds is after washing, pitting, and cutting your fruit up.

Put the cut pieces on a cookie sheet so the pieces *are not touching each other*. Then freeze. Place the frozen fruit into bags and return the bags to the freezer.

In this way, you can pour frozen peach slices into your blender with ease.

One year I cut up peaches and pitted cherries and put them straight into a freezer bag. Unfortunately, they froze into mammoth fruit boulders, and I had to go *Psycho* on them with an ice pick in order to use them. So freeze the pieces separately, otherwise your fruit boulders will still be in your freezer two years later because who wants to be Norman Bates when you're hungry and it's 98 degrees out?

YOU CAN EAT THAT?

"Ever eat a pine tree?"
—EUELL GIBBONS

Before I began eating from the Quarter-Acre Farm, I wondered about the first person who tried eating an artichoke. He must have been desperate. Armored as an armadillo, artichokes seem about as palatable as one as well. The culprit certainly must have been starving and nothing else but the artichoke was growing within crawling distance.

My mother used to fix artichokes only once every year or two. We loved the strange finger food. I have to admit, however, that it wasn't the artichokes we loved, it was being allowed to eat as much Miracle Whip as we wanted. I doubted there was Miracle Whip at the ready for that first bite of artichoke. Desperation indeed.

However, the Quarter-Acre Farm taught me that desperation probably didn't engender that first foray into an artichoke heart—for one thing, artichokes love water and cool temperatures, so they wouldn't have been the only plant around. Instead, education likely inspired those first edible thoughts about artichokes.

We have been schooled into believing that there is a narrow subset of edibles in the world, in our gardens, and *on* each plant. It's what we see when we go into the grocery store. And the reason we don't see more of what is edible in the grocery stores *isn't* because the breadth of edibility is narrow, it's because of ease. The grocery chains purchase food that is:

- easiest to grow in large amounts,
- easiest to douse with insecticides and herbicides,
- easiest to pick and process,
- easiest to ship,
- easiest to store and sell,
- easiest to prepare,
- easiest to get the most money for the least effort.

Sometimes we pay extra for food that has become fashionable (like microgreens or blue potatoes) or somehow touches a place in our collective memory (such as heirloom tomatoes or pattypan squash). But the longer a society goes without eating something, the less likely it is that people will eat it again. Foods aren't lost as much as they fall out of use, and then out of memory (as has been the case with orach, mock oyster, sweet potato leaves, and yellow nutsedge). Not necessarily *entire* foods, either. We either forget how many *parts* of a plant can be eaten or we're fearful of trying them. Some caution is warranted, for not every part of every edible plant *is* edible.

Take rhubarb as one of the most common examples. While the stalks of the plant are prized for their tart-sweet flavor, their leaves have a relatively large amount of a compound called oxalate, which renders them poisonous. Sure, it would take about eleven pounds of rhubarb leaves to make a lethal dose, but it requires much less than that to make you feel ill from eating the stuff—perhaps, say, a mere burning of the mouth, some abdominal pain, and general weakness.

The specter of rhubarb's dire inedibility is so indelibly imprinted on me that the one year I planted rhubarb chard I couldn't bring my-self to eat it, even though I could *see* that it was chard. Since the tiny plants had been labeled merely "rhubarb," I thought perhaps they were a tiny *cultivar* of rhubarb. As they grew, however, I brilliantly thought, "Gee, I never realized how much rhubarb looks like chard." When I ate a bit of the stalk, it wasn't sour; it tasted like chard. Since it looked, tasted, smelled, and grew like chard, I told myself it *must* be chard. But so strong was my aversion to being poisoned (I do consider this a posi-tive character trait), I couldn't bring myself to try the leaves. I eventually went back to the garden center, found the "rhubarb" and fully read the information on the plastic stake, noting the words "rhubarb chard" that had been pushed below the soil line.

Though the *leaf* of rhubarb is poisonous, the stalk is delicious—whether served raw or in jellies, pies, and sauces . . . and the plant has other uses as well. Boiling the stalks in burnt pans will eliminate stains and bring back the pot's original shine. If you simmer rhubarb root in water, you can use the resulting rinse to make blonde or light-brown hair a more golden color. And those pesky leaves? Boil them and use the water for a natural insecticide.

Unfortunately, this sort of whole-plant knowledge is all but history for us now.

Let's revisit that artichoke. . . .

When I started farming the Quarter Acre, I was already growing artichokes, but more for aesthetic than culinary reasons—I love the giant thistly purple flowers that artichokes turn into when they reach full bloom.

By that time, I did appreciate artichokes as more than just mayonnaise spoons, and I very much loved artichoke hearts, but the plant took up a lot of room for not much sustenance. Then I visited my friend Shawna and she offered me some Vietnamese artichoke tea. It was delicious, and more, it was made out of artichoke leaves. Artichoke leaves are *edible?*

As soon as my artichokes were in full leaf, I harvested several of the large, hirsute leaves and dried them in the dehydrator. When they were dried, I readied a tea ball. But just as I was stuffing leaves into the perforated aluminum tea globe, I started wondering, *What if by "artichoke" the makers of that Vietnamese tea were referring to Jerusalem artichokes?* Then I remembered the picture of the fat artichoke on the front of the tea box. They were definitely talking about artichoke. I poured water into the teapot, but as I was about to lower the tea ball into the pot

I thought, *What if by artichoke leaf they meant the artichoke petals?* Over and over again I had seen recipes in which the "petals," the artichoke's armor-like scales, are referred to as leaves. If the artichoke petals can safely be consumed, the leaves assuredly could be too. Or maybe not. I put the tea ball aside. I'd have to look into this more fully.

Finding information about the edibility of plants, and certainly plant *parts,* is not as easy as you'd think, especially if the plant grows in a very small part of the country. (Eighty percent of artichokes in the United States are grown around the Castroville area of California where Marilyn Monroe was crowned the first Artichoke Queen.) The artichokes in the States are used virtually entirely for their buds (and hearts), and so while I found a wealth of information online regarding their nutrition, as well as recipes for cooking the buds, I didn't find much about the rest of the plant. At least the leaves didn't show up on the poisonous plants list. Finally, I typed "Vietnamese artichoke farming" into the search engine and got more information.

I discovered that in Vietnam, artichokes are not grown solely for the bud, but for many uses, including tea. My favorite description came from a Vietnamese website:

> *The Dalat farmers grow artichokes for meals and medicine. The roots, stems, flowers, and leaves of artichokes are used in Dalat medicine. The flower heads are used in Vietnamese soup stewed with meat. The leaves, stems, roots, and flowers are dried under*

the sun and concocted. The resultant refreshing drink is diuretic and provides very good nourishment for humans' liver cells. Artichoke tea is a daily beverage for many Vietnamese villagers.

Other sites celebrated the fact that all of the "organs" of the artichoke could be utilized: *roots and rhizome* for brews or infusions; the *whole plant* as an ornamental in landscaping; the *leaves* for alcoholic drinks, pharmacological products, beauty creams, as a substitute for herbal tea (called tisane), as protein for biscuits and beverages, as a sweetening agent and milk coagulant, and as dehydrated flour in animal feed. The *midribs* can be cooked in a variety of dishes, and the *immature flower heads*, the *receptacle*, and *hearts* can be eaten raw or cooked in more than a thousand recipes, and can even be an ingredient in ice cream. The *mature flower heads* are used in dried flower arrangements, the *seeds* provide oil, and the byproducts of the artichoke are used as fodder for many animals. Even the *stems* can be peeled and eaten like hearts of palm.

And as go artichokes, so go many plants. Everyone knows lemons provide lemon juice and the perfect garnish for ice tea, but how many lemonade lovers also know that lemon peel is edible and gives twice the tart bang for their buck. Further, both beet greens and beetroot are delicious (most people know this, but I hadn't eaten either of them before the Quarter Acre Farm year). Still fewer people probably know that cactus paddles are edible, as well as the round red cactus fruit. If you love broccoli, you will also love broccoli leaves and broccoli stems.

When I was waiting on my garlic to come to full bulb, I could enjoy the garlic leaves (just as you can onion leaves) and garlic "scapes"—the stalk and nascent flower of the developing garlic bulb, which are a real treat. Further, garlic and onion flowers aren't the only treat—so are squash flowers, nasturtiums, rosemary flowers, broccoli flowers, pea flowers, and fava bean blossoms.

Fava bean *leaves* are also edible (and delicious sautéed in olive oil with garlic a la spinach, or served raw in salad) and the young beans can be eaten pod and all. Pea leaves, by the way, are delicious, and when they're served with blossom and tendrils intact they make a loooovely presentation.

So-called weeds are also underutilized. Dandelions were purposely brought across the Atlantic by immigrants (a fact that would make some of my lawn-proud friends gnash their teeth in fury). The new Americans used the leaves and flowers as both food and a medicinal source. Dandelion greens have five times the amount of omega-3 fatty acids as spinach. Dandelion flowers are used in wine, and they make a delicate, honey-like jelly.

Purslane is another ubiquitous weed. It is a "succulent" (a family of hardy, thick-leaved, water-retaining plants that include the cactus) with red stems and fleshy green leaves. It was a terrible embarrassment when I was given seeds to grow a supposed weed and I couldn't manage to foster them. Luckily, they eventually self sowed. If *you* get them to grow, as most humans (and birds for that matter) can, the tart vitamin C-rich plant adds crunch to salads and sandwiches and is rich in omega-3s, minerals, vitamins, and fiber.

When I was a kid, I thought Euell Gibbons was an actor hired by Post Cereal to act like a naturalist who appreciated their cereal, Grape Nuts. But then again, I thought Grape Nuts were actually grape seeds, too. As it happens, Mr. Gibbons really was a naturalist, and you can read his fine books (including his "*Stalking*" series: . . . *the Wild Asparagus, . . . the Blue Eyed Scallop, . . . the Healthful Herb*) to learn a wealth about foods that we overlook every day. He points out that not only do we throw out the tastier and more nutritious crop when we weed purslane from among the spinach plants, but also that we take a wrong-headed approach in seeing these foods merely as possible alternatives to starvation (my fantasy of the artichoke plant). He counsels that we should instead look at the overlooked foods as delicious, meaningful plants that will give you a sense of independence from supermarkets and a deeper relationship with nature.

Emerson wrote, "A weed is a plant whose virtues we have not yet discovered." These days I believe that we can safely enlarge that sentiment to "*Plants* are foods whose virtues we have not yet discovered."

We are, in great numbers, eating foods in which not only virtues have been discovered (a kick-ass secret sauce), but also whose deleterious effects (clogged arteries, heart failure, metabolic disorders, excess fat, cancer) are also well documented.

The next time I want a McDonald's Quarter Pounder, I'm going for the purslane salad tossed with preserved lemon, followed by an artichoke tea chaser, instead.

Sam's Preserved Lemons

Remember that song, "Lemon tree very pretty and the lemon flower is sweet, but the fruit of the poor lemon is impossible to eat . . . " Well, so much for truth in song lyrics, for not only *can* you eat the fruit, but you can eat the *rind* of the lemon as well. Perhaps not straight off the tree, but preserved lemon rind is good. Really, really good. Who would have thought?

We have an old Meyer lemon tree in our yard that with some babying and pruning began bearing beautiful yellow-orange lemons plump with sweetly tart juice and corseted with thin, tender peels. These lemons make wonderful lemonade and are my number one choice for gin and tonics. However, I don't like to use them for preserved lemons.

My preserved lemon of choice is the Eureka lemon. Eureka lemons are huge bruisers. Their juice hits you with a jaw-clenching pucker and their fruit is mattressed within a thick yellow rind. It is a lemon's rind that counts with preserved lemons, for though the lemons are preserved in their entirety, it is only the rind that is used in recipes: the lemon "guts" are discarded. The thick preserved Eureka rinds have *substance*: they are chewy, wildly lemony, somewhat salty, and taste good in practically everything.

It was Sam who first preserved lemons, a result of trying to perfect his chicken piccatta recipe. (He started making the piccata when he was too short to fry the cutlets.) Sam got the instructions from his cooking pal, Sally, who was plenty tall to fry cutlets.

While Sam uses preserved lemons in his piccata, I serve them chopped in salads, in rice, julienned on top of chicken, and as a seasoning in soups and stews. I have even been known to eat them out of the jar, though I've also been caught sipping pickle juice a time or two.

Best of all, not much could be easier than preserving lemons. I do add an extra step, however. While most people feel fine about not heat bathing their jars of preserved lemons, I admit to a dread of killing someone with home canning. So after my lemons are sealed into their jars, I put the jars into a vat of boiling water for ten minutes. After they are drained and cooled I make sure the jar lids have all sealed and then I store them in the dark pantry.

As an additional perk to not killing someone, the hot-water bathing cuts the time until the lemons are ready to eat.

Ingredients:

- several ½ pint to full-pint canning jars (depending on how many you'd like to make)
- 2 or more Eureka lemons (same as with above)
- salt

Use canning jars with a large mouth to facilitate getting the lemons in and out. You'll want enough lemons so that the lemons are packed tightly in the jar(s). Boil the jars and scrub the lemons (some dip their lemons into boiling water to encourage the juice and to make sure they are really clean).

While most people preserve their lemons whole, I like to slice the lemons into ¼ inch thick half-moon slices. I find that not only can I get more into the jar that way, but I can also use any size jar (a couple of whole lemons are difficult to fit into a half-pint jar, and they don't fill a pint jar, but if the two lemons are sliced I can do a quick half-pint of preserved lemons if I need to). Further, the lemon rinds absorb the salt and juice more quickly, and they are easier to use once they are ready.

1. Cut the clean lemons in half from stem to stern then into ¼ inch slices. For each half pint, I figure two medium lemons, then go up from there.

2. Whichever size jar you use, start by sifting a tablespoon of salt in the bottom.

3. Next, layer the bottom with lemons, and sift a thin layer of salt over them. Continue with layering lemon slices and salt until the jar is filled (mushing down the lemons as you go) to a ½-inch below the rim.

4. If there is not enough juice to fill the jar, squeeze some extra juice from a few standby lemons.

5. Seal the jars and place in boiling water. Make sure the water is deep enough to cover the jar by an inch. Let boil for ten minutes before removing the jar and letting it cool.

6. After the jar cools, check for a good seal. If the seal is good, you can push on the top and there will be no click or give. If the seal didn't work, you can discard the lid, put another on, and try again, or merely stick the jar in the refrigerator to use within the next month.

7. I usually wait two weeks before cracking open a jar. When it *is* time, pull out the lemon, rip out and discard the fruit inside, and rinse the rinds of salt.

The rinds are wonderful minced and scattered atop a slab of warm-from-the-garden tomato, some fresh basil, and a few soft pillows of mozzarella. Add them to sautéed baby artichokes with butter or orzo with asparagus, and chop them with green olives for a preserved lemon and olive relish. You'll never sing the lemon tree song without scoffing again.

A FARMER CRITIQUES THE QUARTER ACRE FARM

"Last night there came a frost, which has done great damage to my garden...It is said that Nature will play such tricks on us poor mortals, inviting us with sunny smiles to confide in her, and then, when we are entirely within her power, striking us to the heart."
—NATHANIEL HAWTHORNE, *THE AMERICAN NOTEBOOKS*

Every farmer like me needs to know a farmer like Lloyd Johnson. There is a wealth of information about plants and earth that someone who has brought hundreds of thousands of pounds of produce to fruition can pour into my relatively (sadly) empty vessel of a head. In fact, no matter if someone gardens or farms or not, it would enrich anyone's life to befriend a farmer.

Now, I've long said that *pediatricians* are, overall, fine human beings in a world of sometimes disappointing examples. I think back on all the pediatricians that my children have coughed on, barfed on, screamed and kicked at (Sidney, Jesse is sorry about that incident when he was six), and there are amazingly few that I wouldn't be absolutely thrilled to sit down and talk to over dinner. I'd even buy. And let me be clear—I can't so easily say that about members of any other profession I've come across. Except for farmers.

This parallel kind of makes sense. Farmers and pediatricians are drawn to helping things grow, to keeping an eye on the health of vulnerable entities. They are on call through all hours of day and night in case of freeze or fevers, disease, drought, hunger, weeds, grasshoppers, or head lice. They do this in spite of the other end of things—in spite of parents who freak over low-grade fevers (again, apologies) or feed their kids Big Gulps, or fear, or unhealthy attitudes; they do this in spite of a population that values the cosmetically perfect over healthful growing practices, and in spite of Mother Nature, who can be cruel to beans and babies alike.

Farmers and pediatricians do the work they do because they get satisfaction out of a flavorful tomato, a crisp carrot, a grinning toddler, and a kid whose pink eye cleared up nicely.

Pediatricians, farmers, I thank you.

Unfortunately, not many of us do know farmers. Even if we go to farmers' markets and buy their produce, we generally don't really get to know them. I didn't. I smiled and thanked them for my purchases. These people are *busy*, and what do you say, anyway? I always had the uncomfortable feeling that if I were to start talking vegetables, they might think I was either a complete idiot or trying to ferret out information like those people who go to craft fairs and ask the artists, "How did you make this?" then announce, "Well, I'm not paying fifteen dollars when I can do *that* myself."

So when I got the idea to have a real farmer come to the Quarter Acre Farm, I was nervous about the imposition at the very least. Luckily my future daughter-in-law Nicole worked both as a vintner and at the farmers' market, so she knew farmers who hearkened from one side of the county to the other. When I asked her if she knew of anyone who would be willing to visit my farm, she came up with Lloyd's name right away and said that not only did Lloyd grow the most beautiful organic tomatoes she had ever seen, but that he was also a great guy.

Backing up her claims, Farmer Lloyd readily agreed to make a February visit to the Quarter-Acre Farm.

I was sorry the visit was in winter since the farm wasn't showing as well as it had in summer when the yard burgeoned with fruit and vegetables. In February, it was at its least productive, least attractive. Still, I reasoned that the worse off the Quarter Acre, the more Lloyd Johnson could likely help me, and help was what I wanted after all.

Unfortunately, after Lloyd and I had set the date for the visit, things immediately started to go wrong on the farm, making a poor showing into a disastrous one. We had a freeze, followed the next night by another freeze, and then another. Each freeze weakens a plant's abilities to withstand another frost, so by the time the successive nights of freezes eased, Central Valley farmers had deployed their bag of tricks against the cold, turning fans on in the low areas to blow away the frigid air that pooled like killing gas, or watering into the night to try to ameliorate the cold temps by even a degree or two in hopes it might make a difference. Luckily the frosts did not do terrible damage, only spotty damage. And partially because I found the Quarter Acre Farm too small to merit fans and too large to be covered by tarps, and myself too ignorant to know anything else to do, one of the damaged spots was my yard.

I had hoped my peas would be covering the trellises by the time Farmer Lloyd came to visit, but now that was not to be. Many of my plants had either succumbed entirely to the frost or had left only weasely little stems that were certainly nothing to be proud of. Further, my beets were slow, my cauliflower stunted, and most of my flowers done for, leaves blackening and curling like they had been torched rather than touched by ice.

The general rattiness of the garden horrified me, and because of that horror I had to admit to myself that I wasn't just looking for help. I wanted Farmer Lloyd to pat me on the back, perhaps even accept me as a fellow farmer, even though I only had a relative postage stamp of land to work with. I wanted him to teach me the special farmer's handshake, and *then* introduce me to the club's farming secrets.

That wasn't going to happen; I could see that well enough from my front porch, where I further noticed that my cabbages looked embarrassingly scrawny. I'd developed company eyes.

Our family coined the phrase "company eyes" to describe the phenomena of how the closer it came time for friends to arrive at our home, the more we noticed . . . *things*. Cobwebs glowed in the corners, the crack above the door became a chasm, dust bunnies ran out from under the couch, and the living room looked more like a flea market than a room in which civilized folks resided.

Now having made the appointment with Lloyd, I looked around the garden and saw the truth. I was no more a farmer than I was a brain surgeon. Casting a jaded eye from bed to bed I thought it likely I was closer to being a brain surgeon, for that matter.

Why had I gotten myself into this situation? The trees were ill-pruned, the beets were planted too closely together, the chicken house looked silly, and all those patios! I should have never listened to Louis; we should have ripped them all out. *A serious farmer would have.* At least my broccoli looked good, big heads forming on strong stalks, and the keyhole garden in the back was green with a carpet of mâche and spinach. The rainbow chard was growing vigorously. I tried to take solace in that. What else could I do to prove myself anywhere close to a serious grower?

Potatoes! I could plant my potatoes. That would show him I knew about potatoes (unlike Spring of the failed potatoes from *last* year). I turned the soil in one of the raised beds and dug a trench down the middle. I placed some of my sprouted potatoes in the trench, and then on the raised bed I arranged a tray containing the rest of the sprouts, along with a trowel, as a sort of "still life of a farmer."

I cleaned up—I raked the mulch smooth, uprooted frost-killed plants, and pulled weeds. And even though every self-respecting farm and ranch I had ever been on had its own junk pile that furnished parts in a pinch to repair the tractor, hold back erosion, or cobble together a table on which to feed a work crew, I swore I would tackle Farmer Lloyd before letting him take a look at my side yard. And it was a true junk yard: a pile of fence posts and tarps, a rick of firewood, sections of fence, the defunct snail terrarium, three compost piles, excess sand, two ladders, and an old chair I meant to refinish but was now more suited for kindling. If you ignored the side yard, the place looked tidy—and that was all I had.

Then the wind came up.

In the night the wind rose from a sigh to a bluster. By dawn it was out and out gusting, and by full light it had screamed into a gale. I stood in the early morning with my hair whipping around me, morose over the huge amount of storm flotsam littering the yard, with more ripping from the trees. Shivering in my ratty robe, I went to check the fishpond. The neighbor's towering redwood that creaked and waved in the wind had loosed what seemed like half its dead branches and needles into the once tranquil pool. Now it was a mucky mess that I would have to dredge out if and when the wind stopped.

Disheartened, I traipsed over to the goose yard where Goosteau was honking frantically at the wild weather. Just as I was running my hand over the agitated gander's back, there was a terrific crack and a louder *whomp!* Goosteau and Jeannette lifted from the ground and flew a panicked several yards, the chickens squawked, and I shrieked and spun around. The fishpond was no longer visible. Twelve feet of the top of the neighbor's towering redwood was now covering it *and* the northeast quarter of the backyard.

I should have been giddy—after all, not only had I sidestepped death by a mere seven feet, but I had sidestepped *being found dead in my stained, tattered, twenty-some-year-old robe.* I wasn't giddy however. Instead, all I could think of was the upcoming farmer's visit and the ton of dead tree in the yard. This was not going to help matters *at all.*

Our neighbors rushed over right away and I rushed inside to get dressed. Then our two families began cutting up the tree and carrying the logs and branches out in a de-limbing production line. In two hours, most of the large stuff was cleared out. Unfortunately, my jujube tree had been split in two, the fish pond was now not only filled with redwood flotsam but also sawdust, and the raised bed that had been so prettily green with mâche and spinach was now fully disturbed, plants uprooted, as the limbs of the tree had driven into the soft dirt.

We cleaned up most of the mess before Farmer Lloyd came to visit the next day. I bound the split tree with enough white tape that it looked like it was recuperating from a skiing accident and reset the stones around the raised bed. The uprooted spinach and mache were almost all goners, however, but nothing could be done about that. I was going to have to accept that the visit would be an embarrassment.

The day that Lloyd came to visit was a grey one, as most Northern California days are between February and March (and April and sometimes even into May). But at least it wasn't drizzling. I put on the kettle, and when Lloyd knocked on the door, I invited him in for a cup of tea. He *looked* like a farmer, which wasn't surprising.

While farmers come in every shape, size, sex, color, and creed, it is a pretty safe bet that each one of them, once having spent some time on their farm, is going to have a squint, a tan (though often a perfectly white forehead thanks to the ubiquitous hat), calloused hands, and powerful arms, plus they will move well, at least when they are outside and have some space to move around in. Lloyd had all these attributes. He was a big guy, on the quiet side, with an affable, hesitant smile underneath his beard.

I asked him in and we sat at the table, drank tea and talked, and found we were both artists, had both spent time in Wyoming, and both loved to grow things. Lloyd, however, was a real farmer and I, well . . . after a couple of mugs of tea, it was time to stop the pleasantries, step outside, and show him *what* I was and what I was doing in my yard in the middle of Davis, California.

I told Lloyd that I'd like him to critique the Quarter-Acre Farm for me as if it were a real farm and gave him an example: "For instance, I'll bet if you had that big stump (a large piece of the ornamental cherry my neighbors had cut down and I asked to have dragged to my yard because it looked nice), the first thing you might say is, "Get rid of that thing, it's right in the middle of the tomato patch."

With that, Lloyd nodded and got to work. As all good critiquers do, he threw me a few compliments to start things off. He approved of the fava beans (he called them bell beans) that I had planted, which were already about a foot tall and unimpaired by the frost. He said they were good for fixing nitrogen in the soil and he used them at his own farm as a winter cover crop. He then bent down and took a look at the dirt. He said it looked fine—dark, crumbly, and rich.

I felt the glow I usually felt when someone was complimenting one of my kids. This was going better than I thought! Basking in good feelings over my good dirt and nitrogen-fixing legumes, we then looked at the cabbage and cauliflower patch. They were, with really no other word for it, puny.

Lloyd looked apologetic, much like a teacher charged with telling a student they were going to have to repeat kindergarten. He asked when I had planted the miserable crucifers. I mumbled maybe sometime in late October, maybe early November. Lloyd said the plants were in stasis—planted so late in the season they didn't get enough light for them to really get going. He told me that a good rule of thumb was that the starts for winter crops should be in *before Labor Day.* If you plant by Labor Day, the plants will be providing by Thanksgiving. What I would get now, he told me, was what a friend of his referred to as "bonsai vegetables." And certainly I had already picked a few of the miniature heads of cauliflower that looked more like they were grown by Lilliputians than an average-height woman.

We traipsed into the back and right away Lloyd said raised beds gave him the heebie-jeebies, especially the ones like I had that were wide and high. He said not only did he like to use a tractor or a rototiller on his place, which was impossible in those beds, but you also lost 25 percent of your useable space with raised beds. Worse than that, they were problematic in the summer. Planting in raised beds puts plants up in the air during the torrid weather where their roots were much more likely to get dried out and hot than if they were planted at ground level. Further, he said, it made it difficult, if not impossible, to really water well.

At his farm Lloyd said he practices "deep-watering." *Really* deep watering. Upon first planting his tomatoes, he soaks them with water and then isn't likely to water again for three weeks. His tomatoes might only get watered five times the entire summer. Five times? That's it? I was amazed.

Lloyd then looked around and said the trees were a problem. I admitted to wormy apples. Lloyd said he didn't grow fruit, but that the farm down the way sprayed their apples every ten days with *Bacillus thuringiensis*, a biologic alternative to insecticide. I scribbled notes furiously while Lloyd went on to explain that his problem with my trees was actually the shade. Was there enough sunshine for farm vegetables?

I admitted that I had to be very careful to find the spots that did get over six full hours of light, but once the light shifted in the summer and we had trimmed the branches, there was a surprisingly large area that was bright most of the time.

By this time, Goosteau had seen us and commenced honking at us like five lanes of rush-hour traffic. Lloyd winced and asked, "Your neighbors don't mind this?" He looked like he'd appreciate returning to the peace of the front yard, but I figured I was going to get Lloyd to solve all my problems, so I ignored the noise and told him about my nematode problems with tomatoes and ushered him over to the bug damage on the chard.

Lloyd told me that they were starting to graft heirloom tomatoes to nematode-resistant rootstock, and so maybe in the future I could grow heirlooms after all. As for the other insects, if he really needed plants to be pristine, like basil to sell to the supermarket, he used floating row covers on those crops. Otherwise bugs didn't bug him, it was the weeds that threatened to break the bank. (I was suddenly very glad I'd taken pains to weed when Lloyd looked around and said that wasn't a problem here.)

We talked weeding a bit and he said he had a few tools that were his favorite to work between the rows. If the rototiller wouldn't work, he'd use a stirrup hoe on a wheel. He said he had great control that way and he could nudge in really close to the plants. I asked if he planted through sheet plastic and he said never. He said it took another tool to lay the plastic then to tamp down the edges. Besides, he didn't like plastic, didn't like to buy it or throw it away. I agreed with him, and on that note I thought I'd impress him with my potato savvy, so I led him over to my carefully orchestrated potato-planting still life.

He raised his eyebrows and said it was *kind of early* to be planting potatoes. He liked to plant mid-March. The potatoes would be ready by June. He offered that Lockhart Seeds in Stockton was not only a great place to buy seeds, but they would also give me a good planting chart for this region (obviously my calendar was one of my weak points).

When Lloyd said it was time for him to go, I asked him to come back when the weather changed, intimating that he had caught the Quarter-Acre Farm mid growing stride, and hoping he'd believe that the place could give Eden a run for it's money on the right day. I was still hoping he'd teach me that secret farmer's handshake and figured I had some time between now and then to make changes, pull those bonsai vegetables, plant the summer crop in good time, nix the narrow masonry raised beds, and maybe dig up one of those stirrup hoes he had told me about and thereby prove my chops as a farmer. Further, Lloyd's visit was just the shot in the arm I needed (a sort of spring tonic!) to get excited about growing things all over again.

The next time Lloyd visited it was the first day of summer. He came with his farming and life partner, Sarah, and we walked around the Quarter-Acre Farm. This time there were tomatoes on the vine, pepper plants growing, grapes dangling from the arbor, and the geese were as noisy as ever. The potatoes were ready to be dug (luckily I hadn't ruined them by planting too early), and Lloyd, Sarah, and I compared notes on how many tubers we were getting and how big they were. I admit to feeling just a little bit farmer-y shooting the breeze with Sarah and Lloyd, chewing a piece of green sorrel as the hens clucked and the fruit hung heavy on the trees. Lloyd looked a little puzzled over my onions, however, and when I visited his farm I could see why.

Lloyd's farm was about twenty miles out. A flat six acres with straight rows, most of them a rototiller's distance from the next. He had beans, potatoes, tomatoes, squash, eggplant, herbs, cabbages, basil, and of course, onions. The onions were huge! Not only that, they weren't flowering like mine. We had already ascertained that we had planted at the same time. What the heck?

One reason for the difference in size was also one of the things that set Lloyd's farm apart from mine: water. Lloyd got his water from a deep well. The well was a good one, and the water abundant, cheap, and chlorine free. He worried more about the electricity to pump the water up than he did about the water itself.

At the Quarter-Acre Farm I was always being stingy with water because town water was expensive. While Lloyd laved his farm with water, deluging certain areas until they were flooded, and again when they dried, I tended to underwater instead. And my onions reflected it. But that wasn't the only reason for the differences in our onions. Lloyd started his onions from seed.

He explained that onions were biennials. During the first year growing, they produced bulbs then went dormant over the winter. In the spring, they roused again to grow a bit more, put out flowers, and then seed. I hadn't grown my onions from seed. I grew them from the little clove-like bulbs called "onion sets" that I got in a net bag at the garden store.

Apparently that was the problem. It was Lloyd's experience that those little sets practically ensured your onions would bolt. He didn't know exactly how they got the onions to produce those little bulbs, but it seemed that once planted, the onions considered themselves in their second-year growth pattern.

You learn something new every day.

We walked through the rows of produce then went into the shed to consider the famous wheeled stirrup hoe. Lloyd took down a hand-held hoe he'd gotten for a song at a place in Woodland. He showed me how the family that owned the place welded old disc blades into well-balanced hoes with a really good heft. The scar from the weld was neat and uniformly ribbed—a skilled job. They'd obviously made a lot of them. Lloyd liked the hoes not only because they were solid, but also for the idea that the disc blades were made in some distant place, but re-made into this simple good tool there in Woodland. I understood completely.

I figured it was kind of like planting a seed or grafting a limb. Lloyd and I had both worked with ceramics, so maybe it was that mud-to-mug feeling—using what was seemingly worthless to make something useful and well balanced. Once again I enjoyed that good fellow-farmer feeling. But even as I indulged myself in that camaraderie, I knew better than to imagine we two farmers were doing the same thing—at all.

This knowledge was brought home about a month later when I rolled my foot while running and broke the fifth metatarsal in my foot. It so happened that I did so while Louis and Sam were out of town for ten days and I was alone at the Quarter-Acre Farm. My foot swollen, tender, and demanding total rest, I found myself benched. Seeming to sense a window of opportunity, Thalia the hen managed to literally fly the coop and headed for the sweet potatoes to dig for worms. I caught sight of her and tottered outside as quickly as I could with my crutches, weaving and tripping on the uneven ground. I got the hen imprisoned once again only to catch sight of the new peppers, which weren't on the drip system. I dragged the hose out to water the desperately wilted plants and almost fell over a raised bed. I got the peppers watered, then remembered I needed to put the next row of beans in . . . but then I snagged my crutch on the hose and barely caught myself from taking a nosedive.

Reeling, my heart pounding at the near miss, I thought how stupid I would feel if I worsened the metatarsal break and had to have surgery—and all in order to save some sweet potatoes and pepper plants. That would be stupid, indeed. I turned off the hose and went inside.

I could do that on the Quarter-Acre Farm because though I was feeding myself and my family with what I grew, I could, if I had to, buy sweet potatoes in the fall, or do without them altogether. We'd be fine. If, however, I depended on that crop to make the payment on the land, or the tractor, or to buy next year's seed or irrigation pipe, then the escaped livestock and the dying produce would be much larger and more serious problems.

I don't have the same consequences of failure that a larger farm does. My losses are a dollhouse mirror's reflection of a regular farm.

Yet that truncated risk is why *the gamble is within reach for most of us.* And why someone who doesn't know much about gardening can weather the ups and downs of learning to grow their own food. The learning curve is steep, but it isn't expensive. However, it would certainly be nice if we *all* had a Farmer Lloyd in our lives to counsel us on hull-less oats, growing onions, and the calendar of planting.

Maybe we could hire farmers in a program where a farmer would always be on call to answer frantic questions about raising tender things to full growth, feeding them, and preventing disease, one who knew when it was right to intervene and when it was right to let growth happen on it's own. To counsel on nutrition, balance, and how much sunshine is required. To recommend books and tools and skills . . . and give knowledgeable advice—just like a pediatrician.

Onion Potato Puff Pastry Pie

It was Lloyd's beautiful torpedo onions that gave me the idea to combine them with my (finally larger than a ping pong ball) potatoes. The onions were the color of merlot and their shape was reminiscent of . . . torpedoes, perhaps, but more the old-fashioned Indian juggling clubs of the Victorian era. Each one weighed over a pound and felt like it would make a decent weapon should I be faced with a home invasion as I made dinner.

Ingredients:

- 2 red onions
- 2 medium potatoes
- 1 sheet puff pastry, thawed
- 2 TB fresh marjoram
- ⅛ cup shredded Romano cheese
- 2 TB olive oil

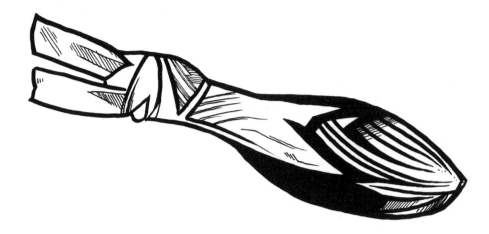

1. Slice the onions, first in half and then into demi-lune slices, enough to fill a 12-inch fry pan.

2. Add the olive oil and heat the skillet on a medium burner. In short order the onions will begin to sweat and wilt and smell wonderful. Give the onions a stir every few minutes and within 20 minutes they'll reduce to a sticky, fragrant, whiskey-colored fraction of their original mass.

3. In the meantime, put the sheet of thawed puff pastry (I admit to buying mine in the freezer section) on a sheet of parchment paper on a cookie sheet and roll it a bit thinner, to about 1/16 of an inch thick, score a line a half inch around the perimeter (like a frame), and jab holes inside that frame with a fork. This allows the frame to puff up while keeping the interior from puffing too much.

4. Boil the potatoes until they are just tender then slice them into 1/8-inch-thick rounds. Put a layer of the potatoes on the puff pastry (inside the frame) and sprinkle with fresh marjoram.

5. Top the potatoes with the caramelized onion and scatter the shredded Romano over the top.

6. Put the whole shebang in a 400-degree oven for 20 minutes.

Oh, this is good. Potatoes, onions, and pastry make for a substantial meal, and since both onions and potatoes store exceedingly well (if they're treated right), this meal can be enjoyed from one season to the next. Lloyd and Sarah sure know how to grow onions. And I have to say, my potatoes weren't too bad either.

VICTORY IN THE GARDEN

*"To forget how to dig the earth and
to tend the soil is to forget ourselves"*
—MAHATMA GANDHI

When I first began the Quarter-Acre Farm experiment, I expected that at the end of the first year I would do something big to honor the endeavor. Maybe I would have a wild bash to celebrate my freedom from the onerous grow-your-own route I had taken. Certainly, when I first started digging out the lawn, digging in seedlings, and digging zucchini for dinner day in and day out, I had envisioned such a party. After all, I figured if I made it through the year, it would be an occasion akin to landing on the moon.

At year's end, I *did,* with great delight, take the kitchen scale off the counter and put it in the lowest drawer next to all the plastics in my Rubbermaid purgatory; I also removed the notebook in which I'd written down everything I'd eaten and how much it weighed for an entire year. That first night, I giddily wolfed down my favorite Mexican take-out food—a meal that I wouldn't *have* to balance with two cucumbers, three tomatoes, eggplant, zucchini, and half a dozen figs. And I once again relished eating cherries I didn't need to weigh first.

In general, however, the end of that seminal year had a genuinely anticlimactic feeling to it. Growing our own food no longer felt Apollo 12-big. Instead it was just something we *did*. It was a little different, but so was the fact that I'd made a lot of the furniture in our house. Different, but hardly noteworthy.

The Quarter-Acre Farm had become a habit.

The more I thought about our Quarter-Acre Farm habit itself, the more I started thinking that of all the things I did on the farm, making a habit out of growing our own food *was* the biggest thing I had done. Especially considering that I was a person woefully deficient in willpower. Heck, most of my farming was done in my tatty but cozy twenty-year-old robe, because I knew if I went inside to change I'd find an excuse to eat something, call someone, or work on that novel before attending to the plethora of weeds choking the eggplants to death.

Habit. The feeling of having it integrated into my life was akin to how I felt when I bowled a strike: I had *no* idea how I'd done it. So I did a little research on the science of habit.

It is an accepted rule of thumb that a habit takes thirty days to make or to break. Actually, it is more a *rule of limb*. In the 1960s, a surgeon by the name of Dr. Maxwell Maltz observed that it took around a month for a person to adjust to the loss of a limb, and he extrapolated that thirty days was therefore the time it took to make any practice into a habit. This thirty-day theory remains widely believed and is one of the reasons that various industries yet announce "Free 30-day trial offers" in hopes of snaring customers into long-term use.

Thirty days seemed pretty optimistic to me, a one-time thumb suck-er who *remembers to this day* the long torment (the shaming, the scolding, the lead-based merthiolate that likely lost me all those brain cells I could really use right now) of breaking that habit. As it happens, I guessed right. There have been further studies into the science of habit in the last fifty years. European researcher Phillippa Lally found that on average it took sixty-six days for an action to be carried to what she called "automaticity." (She also found, understandably, that a plateau was reached more quickly when one was trying to make a habit out of something more pleasant, like drinking a glass of water with a meal versus trying to do fifty sit-ups a day, or perhaps even giving up the tender solace of the thumb.)

I tried to remember when growing, preparing, and eating our homegrown food became automatic for our family. It certainly wasn't within the thirty-day trial offer period. At thirty days in I was still eating zucchini—morning, noon, and night—and Louis and Sam were under-standably refusing to take part in the experiment at all.

I knew the Quarter-Acre Farm was a habit for me before it had be-come habit for Louis, however. I knew this because of the canned tomato incident the winter of that first year.

I had a particularly long day, and Louis offered to make dinner. He makes a great marinara sauce. When I came home, I found cans of tomato sauce and cans of diced tomatoes on our counter—*store-bought* cans, when we had a freezer full of homegrown tomatoes and homemade tomato sauce in the garage!

He explained himself by saying he'd learned to make his marinara using canned tomatoes. He said it didn't occur to him to do anything different.

After I shook bags of icy tomatoes at him with the zeal of a flamenco dancer, I had a feeling that now it might not occur to him to make dinner for me again, at all. Further, there was likely a better way to help make Quarter-Acre Farm produce as much of a habit for him as it seemed canned tomatoes were.

Scientists advise it helps to fit a new habit inside of an already established pattern (rather than performing a punitive tomato fandango, say). As the cook in the family, I'd become used to wandering out into the garden and looking to see what was ripe, then picking what I needed either from the beds or from the freezer. This new habit of "garden shopping" was sandwiched between the hungry howls of the family, "What's for dinner?!" and the actual cooking of that dinner. Of course, Louis and Sam were only doing the howling and eating (and the dishes), and so, though by winter they were happily eating Quarter-Acre produce as most of their diet, it was a passive practice.

Therefore, though I remained the main cook and the main farmer, I began asking the guys to please go out and pick the elements of dinner. At first they weren't really sure which plants were spinach and which were chard. But they were experts in no time.

Sometime later, I asked them both if they would still grow their own food if I weren't around. (Jesse, of course, *does* grow his vegetables, but at his own place.) Both Louis and Sam failed to say they'd find it impossible to ever eat again if something happened to me, and instead they gave me a cheerfully certain reply that yes, they would grow their own food.

Sam said he would especially grow his own tomatoes. He'd noticed that the ones we purchased at the grocery store were not nearly as good as the home-grown variety, and further, were very expensive. He pointed out that a small box of organic cherry tomatoes cost "over four dollars," no doubt tallying up just how many hundreds of dollars of tomatoes he consumed in one tomato season.

Another way I tried to habituate the guys to growing and eating our own food was to borrow from the National War Gardening Commission, circa 1917. The commission was the brainchild of Charles Lathrop Pack to bring together national and local resources for home gardeners. The first order of business was to make a patriotic call to arms to American citizens, asking them to build a garden. The commission printed posters, including one depicting a raven-haired beauty courting melanoma by desultorily sowing seeds into tilled land while wearing a halter dress fashioned out of the American Flag. (Try wearing that now and see if you don't catch it for abusing the flag.) The credo was "Will you have a part in Victory?" and the slightly alarming, "Every garden a munitions plant."

But I think the most alarming poster was the one that stated, "You can *can* fruits, vegetables, and the Kaiser, too!" There is a bizarre (and not a little gruesome) image of two wholesome-looking mason jars filled with tomatoes and peas, and another jar as well—one that has the head of Kaiser Wilhelm II (and perhaps some of his more nutritious organs) stuffed into it. Wow.

The commission also stirred the nation to put idle ground to use ("slacker lands," as they were called), and used a children's rhyme to illustrate that all the small plots could make a huge difference. "Little drops of water, little grains of sand / Make the mighty ocean and the pleasant land."

That was such a good idea, I tried making up some rhymes for our family.

"*Tender little carrots, juicy clumps of grapes, make a healthy body in a better shape.*"

"*Every time you pick some fruit and every time you eat them, you're saving quarts of ugly crude from contaminatin' Eden.*"

And finally my favorite:

"*Grow a bean, pick a bean, and eat a bean for dinner, use and make gas of your own while getting strong and thinner.*"

You can imagine how these went over, and I promptly reined in my poetic impulses. Perhaps rhymed encouragement was an idea whose time had come . . . and gone.

The War Garden Commission did more than make up creative posters and ditties, however. They taught citizens how to garden, guiding urban farmers with the most basic information, from planting seeds all the way through to how they could utilize and conserve the food they grew.

The commission also helped organize neighborhood and citywide support groups so that gardeners could consult each other about their problems *and* solutions. Victory gardeners did not feel alone in their efforts.

A year gone by in the Quarter-Acre Farm and I wondered if *my* family felt alone in the Quarter-Acre Farm life. I remembered a friend's story about being a child in the sixties and thinking her family members were the only ones eating weird food like millet pancakes.

Did my family feel like lonely millet eaters? I decided to ask them a few questions now that the first year of the Quarter-Acre Farm was over, a sort of benign exit interview . . . without the exit, of course.

Not only did I want to know if they felt that living off the farm was alienating but also what they considered good or bad about the experience. I assured them there didn't *have* to be anything bad. I was very open to their opinion that it was all an *exhilarating, life-changing experience* that they'd like to thank me for.

On the plus side, neither of the guys felt it was alienating. Sam did say his friends thought it novel that he showed up with snails for lunch one day, and Louis indicated that some might think that he was married to a "crazy hippy woman" . . . but generally they considered the farm an experience that had enlarged their lives.

We had all noticed that food and gardening people seemed to automatically draw toward each other. So much so that I started wondering if maybe it was the shared activity of composting that was responsible for a wafting pheromonic call to other gardeners. In any case, between slow food events, neighborhood gardeners, and introductions made on the basis of our Quarter-Acre Farm experience (these usually began with "Listen to what she's doing. . . .") we met many people we would not have met otherwise.

Even though meeting people was great, the best thing about the farm was the food. Sam and Louis said our homegrown food tasted better. Sam, a kid who can be found on most summer days grazing on fruit and vegetables in the yard, said he now felt a little trepidation when he looked at grocery-chain food: "I don't know what's on it, or what's been done to it."

Louis said he now also thought more about the residual impurities in produce and also felt less tolerant of it. "There are complex natural systems out there, but very simple ways to utilize them, such as line catching wild salmon, or growing vegetables using mulch and beneficial insects rather than insecticides and herbicides. Now I think there's less reason to put up with toxic methods."

By now I was feeling pretty good, understanding that the Quarter-Acre Farm was a great experience for my family, right up there with winning the lottery (had we only won the lottery, of course). But I was yet worried about the other shoe falling. I knew growing our own food had its, lets say *difficult*, days and I had just read an article about a family who decided they'd rather eat Big Mac's every day for the rest of their lives than hoe another row. I did sympathize. (I still have dreams of Ho Hos wrapped in their beautiful silver wrappings, so easily available it was as if the Gods on Olympus had tossed them down in a box to reward me for good behavior.) Therefore, I knew I had to ask, but I thought I'd frame the question in a positive way. "So . . . nothing negative to say about The Quarter-Acre Farm experience, I take it?"

Sam said, "Oh, sure. There was some bad stuff."

So much for the lottery.

He continued. "Being guilted into weeding."

I was about to protest, but facts are facts. "Anything else?" I asked.

As Sam does the dishes at our house, he pointed out, "The kitchen was messier. There was dirt attached to everything you dug up, where store-bought food comes with the mud washed off."

True.

I asked Louis the next morning if he had anything bad to say about the farm. He said the worst was the water bill before I figured out the watering system and put timers on everything. "We're paying a residential water rate for agricultural use." Then he amended, "But we're spending less on groceries now as well, and we used a lot of water on our lawn." He mused, "The lawn didn't look so good when we had it either. It was a lot of work, and we didn't get to eat it at the end."

This gave me the in I was looking for. "Sounds like you thought the Quarter Acre Farm was a success.

"Uh-huh."

"It gives us good food, isn't really much more work than keeping a lawn and shrubs manicured, saves money, makes friends, improves the world."

He gave me a look. Oh, he realized where I was going, but now I had him cornered. I sweetly asked, "Guess I was right about it all, wasn't I?"

"All?" he hedged, then admitted, "Yes, you were right about the Quarter-Acre Farm. We not only didn't starve, we ate great food, and I do think the yard is more beautiful than it's ever been."

With that I smiled and put the clippers in my robe pocket and went outside to clip some strawberries for breakfast.

As I searched for the ripe berries, I thought about the day a small neighbor came by, one of the three-foot-tall, four-year-old variety. We were picking strawberries together and after he plucked a berry from its tether and ate it, he asked, "Did you get these from the grocery store?" I said, "No, sweetie, they just grow that way." He was floored. I understood completely how much more amazing it was to have something like a strawberry just materialize than it would be to buy strawberries and somehow affix the fruit to a strawberry plant.

I thought of the scene at the end of *The Great Gatsby*, when narrator Nick Carraway imagines that the Dutch sailors who first sailed into the Hudson River and saw the "fresh green breast of the new world" were gazing upon the last thing left in the world "commensurate to [their] capacity for wonder." I believe, however, that our capacity for wonder is proportional to our capacity for taking care of and paying attention to new worlds that might just wait at the toe of our own front steps.

Breakfast berries now in hand, I looked around the tiny patch of dirt we call the Quarter-Acre Farm. I breathed the scent of tomato, new garlic, and the cool smell of rain-soaked soil. An albatross mosquito-hawk bounced through the air, all filament legs and mica wings. Jewel-bright ladybird beetles hunted aphids alongside thrillingly fast praying mantises. I reached down and tossed a meandering snail to the highly excitable and appreciative ducks and thought about all the things that hum and crawl and fly in the Quarter-Acre Farm. The cats kept me company too, watching our domesticated flock through narrowed eyes as they did the many wild birds—jays, magpies, juncos, hawks, egrets, wrens, brilliant little canaries, and big-breasted mourning doves—who jockeyed for their piece of the farm's wealth as well.

As I watched the mockingbirds perform a fan dance between the rows of tomatoes and beans, I wondered again why I didn't have a party at the end of my year. I pondered this, as I observed a carpenter bee rumbling by like a tiny dirigible and a scrub jay tapping a peanut into the mulch. In the mud beside the pond I saw a fresh opossum print, then noticed that the overhanging apples in the tree alongside were almost ripe. A squirrel scolded, the hens announced an egg, and that's when it hit me: After more than a year of eating out of my yard, in awe of the amount of life abounding in this small garden, I knew why I hadn't had a party. I didn't feel like the Quarter-Acre Farm experiment was ending. I'd barely scratched its heavily mulched surface—there was much more to do, so much more to learn! The Quarter Acre Farm had just begun.

In that light, I mused, perhaps a party was in order after all.

Getting Started

As a writer and an artist I guess it isn't surprising that when I decided to transform my yard into a farm I began by drawing pictures, making lists, and taking copious notes. I have a number of old lab notebooks a friend gave me, and these have become my garden journals. In them I write down a sort of journalism of gardening: what I want to plant, where I want to plant it, when I should plant it, and why it worked, (or why I think it didn't and what to do about it)—as well as lists of what to do both in the short term (today/this week) and long term (this month/year).

In my notebooks, this is in no particular order. The lack of order does make things hard to look up, and I do plan, one of these days, (ha!) to compile my notebooks and rearrange them into something more efficiently informative. You might want to start out with more order, creating various sections for your journal, and sidestep such a necessity.

Garden Plan

Sketch out your garden – it doesn't have to be fancy or exact (though a general correctness of proportion helps) but if you make a drawing of just the permanent parts of your garden—the trees, patios, walkways, shrubs, and driveway—you can copy the sketch each new season, then mark what you plant in the beds.

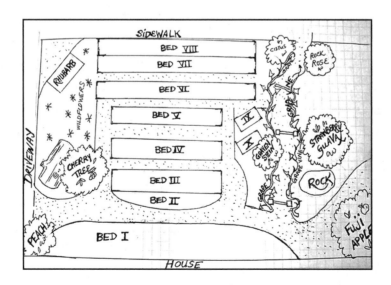

MY GARDEN PLAN

Food

Think of your garden like a future grocery store and make a list of the fruits and vegetables you like to eat:

_____

_____

_____

_____

_____

_____

_____

_____

Planting

Google the planting calendar for your area. This will tell you which of your chosen vegetables should be planted when. Buy the seeds or seedlings for the season you are planting in. Look on the back of the seed packet for time to maturity (harvest). My planting list looked like this for April:

April Planting

PLANT: Cranberry Beans
LOCATION: Beds IV and V
DAYS UNTIL HARVEST: 60 days (mid-June)

PLANT: Golden Beets
LOCATION: Bed I, north side
DAYS UNTIL HARVEST: 55 days (early June)

PLANT: Armenian Cucumbers (start inside)

LOCATION: Bed VI

DAYS UNTIL HARVEST: 135 days (late June)

PLANT: Tomatoes (seedlings, variety)

LOCATION: TBD

DAYS UNTIL HARVEST: 3 months (July 1)

Planting List for my first month:

PLANT: _____

LOCATION: _____

DAYS UNTIL HARVEST: _____

PLANT: _____

LOCATION: _____

DAYS UNTIL HARVEST: _____

PLANT: _____

LOCATION: _____

DAYS UNTIL HARVEST: _____

PLANT: _____

LOCATION: _____

DAYS UNTIL HARVEST: _____

PLANT: _____

LOCATION: _____

DAYS UNTIL HARVEST: _____

Harvest

It's great to note when you were able to harvest the first tomato, the first apricot, the first fava bean. It will be of help for planning next year's garden as well as knowing when to pick your fruit. I can look in my notebook and see that although my oranges look ready in mid November, I know they will not be sweet until Christmas:

PLANT: Navel Orange
DATE READY: first sweet orange December 30, 2009

PLANT: Tomatoes
DATE READY: The first Early Girl was June 24

The first cherry tomato (Sweet Million) June 7

Recipes

Fruits and vegetables that come ripe at the same time, taste great together (Pumpkin and sage, apples and walnuts, tomatoes and cucumbers). This makes it a little easier to cook straight out of the garden. I like to go outside around dinnertime and come up with a recipe using what's ripe on the Quarter Acre Farm. Sometimes the recipe is as simple as sautéing vegetables and tossing them with pasta; sometimes it is a little more of a challenge. If you are anything like me, it is imperative to write the recipe down. No matter if I'm sure I'll remember what I made, I'll actually be lucky if I remembered that I cooked at all:

DATE: March 17th

AVAILABLE IN THE GARDEN: snap peas, onions, thyme, sorrel, eggs

RECIPE: Sorrel/snap pea frittata with strips of red pepper (freezer)

Notes

A good number of pages in my journal are filled with lists of things to do in the garden. While I've got a pen in hand, I then make some notes about what's growing, or how the squirrels are eating the almonds, or the way the chickens scratch like they've learned dance steps. I like to go back to read what was happening a year ago, or two, and I'm always gratified to find that eventually I did accomplish the jobs on my list, even if it did take me a while.

June 14

Picked ½# cherry tomatoes last night for dinner — had them with grilled zucchini

This week

- ○ Trim herb garden
- ○ Pull spent flowers
- ○ Plant DILL!
- ○ Plant Salvia
- ○ Pick chickpeas
- ○ Prune lemon
- ○ Tie tomatoes
- ○ WEED WEED WEED
- ○ Water guava
- ○ Stack raised beds
- ○ NEW CHICKEN PERCH
- ○ mulch Path
- ○ cut artichokes
- ○ Buy twine

Notes on the start of my garden:

July 3

7:30 PM

7:30 AM

2"

My Cowpeas are GROWING! It is amazing how much they grew in 12 hrs. At 7:30 all I could see in the dirt were 2 pale green bridges and by evening most were up in both beds and some of them were two inches tall.

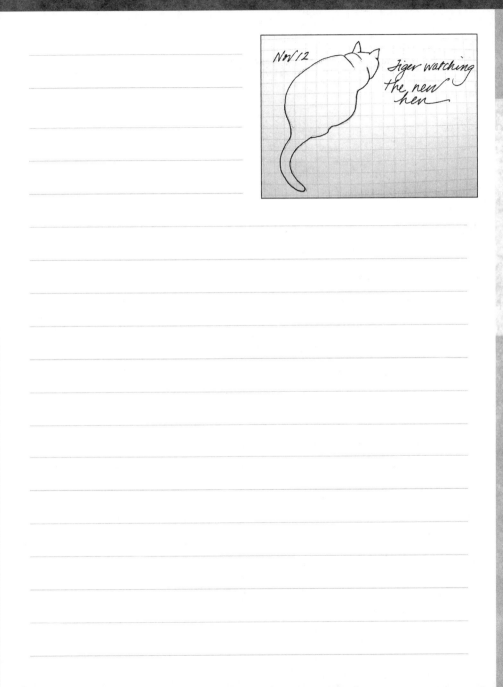

Nov 12

Tiger watching the new hen

ACKNOWLEDGMENTS

I know that I will forget to include someone in this long list of people I am grateful to. Unfortunately, and most likely, the person I forget will be someone of utmost importance. Let me apologize to you in advance.

For the rest I had an idea that I would categorize people and thank them in groups, such as "readers," "editors," "mentors," "family," "neighbors," "friends-who-lent-me-books-or-bought-me-whiskey." However, there was far too much overlap for such a system to work. Instead, I'll start with "A."

Thank you, Emily Albu and Alan Taylor, for tomatoes, wine, root beer, and happy travels. Thank you to my neighbors who have put up with a farm in the neighborhood and the goose noise that goes with it, especially Elaine and Richard, who bear the brunt of the honking, and Laura, Phil, Siena, and Daniel Cox who helped out in so many ways, including providing me with a freezer when I was in great need of it, and a charming weeder (Daniel) on my birthday. Thanks to Judith and Terry for the lemons, Jay for the gardening help, the Chertoks for the orange sticks, and Kate Scow for her soil science expertise.

Thanks to Krista Lyons, Domini Dragoone, Andie East, Merrik Bush-Pirkle, and all of the people at Seal Press for making *The Quarter-Acre Farm* the best it could be. Thanks to Angie Ehrdrich for teaching me about purslane, Dan and Sheri Fields for the talented chickens, to Melissa Franke for introducing me to roasted tomato sauce, and to Laura Gross who is that rarified individual who can be both a spectacular agent and a spectacular friend. Thanks to Lloyd and Sarah Johnson who have patiently taught me about the farming life.

Thanks to Ari and Leslie Kelman, Gail Schneider, and David Matlin not only for friendship but also for being such huge supporters of the Quarter-Acre Farm idea from the very beginning.

Thanks to Marie Lee for being a great writing pal—we will end up at a retreat together sometime soon—and to John Lescroart and Lisa Sawyer for being stellar mentors and friends. I most certainly would not have gotten far without you. Thank you cheese muse Sacha Loren, and thank you to my Sallys—Sally Madden the computer genius and fellow discontent, and Sally McKee the writer and historian who throws a great party, cooks like a maniac, and who also introduced me to Roxanne O'Brien who I thank for her culinary expertise as well.

I want to thank Mike Madison, yet another farmer with a generous heart, for reading QAF chapters; Josie Moody, the best niece in the entire world, for sharing writing with me; Deb Nemier for the keyhole garden idea, Roxy O'Brien for reading my recipes, Dr. Barbara Renwick for reassuring Louis about his wife's health, Chris Reynolds and Alessa

Johns for providing me with books and delightful dinners, Gingy Scharff for her gardening acumen and historical perspective, and Steve Shapson for sharing his mushroom expertise.

Thanks to Carol Kirshnit and Paul Siegel for counsel, latkes, and the fruit of the vine; to Joannie and Clay Siegler for all your help and the best walnuts on the planet; Chuck Krause for seeds and plants, and Deb Neimeier for keyhole gardens.

Thanks to Gary Snyder for sharing the poetry of a handmade life.

Loud and long thank yous to all of the Streeters—my mother and father, Mary and Bob; my sister, Summer; and my brother, Nathan—for appearing in this book again and again, and for loving me even though I am the middle child and now a tattle-tale.

Thank you Diane Ullman for being one of the fantasy sisters and teaching me about bugs, Deb Vanderlist, a fellow small scale farmer, and Eileen Rendahl and Andy Wallace, who most definitely aren't. Also, Eileen . . . just forever thanks. From writing stuff to kid stuff, broken ankles and ailing cats, there are too many ways I depend on you to list here.

Shawna Yang Ryan—I can't imagine being a writer without you there to scheme with, complain to, to ask for edits from, and to celebrate with. And if we weren't writers, we would still be fast friends.

Thank you Yaddo for not only a wonderful place to write, but for inviting the most amazing writers to come at the same time I did. Thanks also to the beautiful Ucross Foundation for the time to write in Wyoming, and finally to the Mesa Refuge, where I put the final edits on the book and tested the QAF recipes on gracious tasters Peter Barnes, Jacob and Gail Needleman, and David Sassoon.

Of course, those that I am most grateful to are my guys. They have all contributed hugely to this effort. Sam was one of my editors, an epicurean of high standards, a fellow animal lover (and wrangler), and a convert to the QAF. Jesse not only illustrated the book but also provided lots of help on the farm, from physical labor to artistic sensibility to horticultural expertise. Further, he brought the darling Nicole into our fold, who knows food and farming and makes a lovely bottle of wine. I couldn't ask for better kids.

As for Louis: while he wasn't always a good sport about the Quarter-Acre Farm, he is *always* a good sport about me *telling* people he wasn't a good sport. He was my first reader, an indispensable editor, and a smart critic. He is also a mulch mover of the highest order and a great weeder. He really does love our little farm underneath it all.

ABOUT THE AUTHOR

Spring Warren was born in Casper Wyoming to parents who designed water treatment plants for a living but also managed to spin wool, throw pottery, and name each of their three children after seasons. Spring graduated from Black Hills State College in Spearfish, South Dakota, and she received an M.A. in Creative Writing from the University of California, Davis. Her novel *Turpentine* (Grove Atlantic, 2008), won the bronze medal in *ForeWord Magazine's* Book of the Year for Historic Fiction, was a recommended title of the New York Center for Independent Publishing, and was a Barnes and Noble Discover Great New Writers selection.

INDEX

SELECTED TITLES FROM SEAL PRESS

For more than thirty years, Seal Press has published groundbreaking books. By women. For women.

DIRT: The Quirks, Habits, and Passions of Keeping House, edited by Mindy Lewis. $15.95, 978-1-58005-261-0. From grime, to clutter, to spit-clean—writers share their amusing relationships with dirt.

Marie's Home Improvement Guide, by Marie L. Leonard. $16.95, 978-1-58005-292-4. A practical how-to guide for women with to-do lists, *Marie's Home Improvement Guide* offers all the tips you need to tackle home repair projects . . . yourself!

Marrying George Clooney: Confessions from a Midlife Crisis, by Amy Ferris. $16.95, 978-1-58005-297-9. In this candid look at menopause, Amy Ferris chronicles every one of her funny, sad, hysterical, down and dirty, and raw to the bones insomnia-fueled stories.

She-Smoke: BBQ Basics for Women, by Julie Reinhardt. $16.95, 978-1-58005-284-9. The owner of Smokin' Pete's BBQ in Seattle lays down all the delicious facts for women who aspire to be BBQ queens.

Pretty Neat: The Buttoned-Up Way to Get Organized and Let Go of Perfection, by Alicia Rockmore and Sarah Welch. $14.95, 978-1-58005-309-9. Funny, irreverent, entertaining, and helpful, *Pretty Neat* offers readers unorthodox, surprisingly simple methods to reduce clutter-induced stress, and insists that perfection is impossible—and unnecessary—in this messy, unpredictable world called real life.

How to Cook a Dragon: Living, Loving, and Eating in China, by Linda Furiya. $16.95, 1-58005-255-X. Part insightful memoir, part authentic cookbook, *How to Cook a Dragon* is a revealing look at race, love, and food in China from *Bento Box in the Heartland* author Linda Furiya.

FIND SEAL PRESS ONLINE
www.SealPress.com
www.Facebook.com/SealPress
Twitter: @SealPress

3 1901 05234 0520